Answers and Hope
for the Struggling Christian

Answers and **Hope** for the **Struggling Christian**

HENRY WARKENTIN

Belleville, Ontario, Canada

ANSWERS AND HOPE FOR THE STRUGGLING CHRISTIAN
Copyright © 2001, Henry Warkentin

All Scripture quotations, unless otherwise specified, are from *The Holy Bible, King James Version.* Copyright © 1977, 1984, Thomas Nelson Inc., Publishers.

Scripture verses marked NIV are taken from the HOLY BIBLE, NEW INTERNATIONAL VERSION ®. Copyright © 1973, 1978, 1984 by International Bible Society. Used by permission of Zondervan Publishing House. All rights reserved.

ISBN: 1-55306-244-2

First printing, June 2001
Second printing, August 2002

**For more information or
to order additional copies, please contact:**

Henry Warkentin
Box 100
Caroline, AB Canada
T0M 0M0

Essence Publishing is a Christian Book Publisher dedicated to furthering the work of Christ through the written word. *Guardian Books* is an imprint of *Essence Publishing.* For more information, contact:
44 Moira Street West, Belleville, Ontario, Canada K8P 1S3.
Phone: 1-800-238-6376 Fax: (613) 962-3055
E-mail: info@essencegroup.com
Internet: www.essencegroup.com

To my wife, Nettie;
To our four children and their families;
And to those who are seeking a closer
walk with God.

TABLE OF CONTENTS

Acknowledgements 9
Introduction 11
1. The Biblical Exposure of the Devil 17
2. Deliverance in the Ministry of Jesus. 25
3. How I Began 41
4. Exposing the Enemy 51
5. Body, Soul, and Spirit 59
6. Seven Steps to Freedom. 86
7. Choosing God's Perspective. 92
8. Freedom from Rejection and Rebellion 117
9. God Actually Uses the Enemy 126
10. Depending on God. 165
11. The Exchanged Life. 175
Notes. 203

ACKNOWLEDGEMENTS

I AM DEEPLY GRATEFUL TO my wife, Nettie, and our four children and their spouses for their help and encouragement to write this book. I am also grateful to my many friends for their support and assistance. I thank the many counselees who experienced freedom from bondage, and who encouraged me to put in writing the truths that had helped them, so they could review them and also pass them on to others. This is my attempt to fulfill that request.

These are not principles that I have just studied and memorized, and then passed them on. Rather, God has birthed them in me, and they have become life to me. Above all, I thank God for the privilege He has given me to witness the miraculous changes in many people as they grasped the truth of God and rejected the lies of Satan.

Henry Warkentin

INTRODUCTION

◆

THE BIBLE SAYS, *"And you shall know the truth and the truth shall make you free"* (John 8:32). Therefore, it must follow that if we are in bondage in any area, we are believing lies in that area. Eve's episode in the Garden of Eden illustrates this clearly. As long as Adam and Eve were agreeing with the truth God had given them, they were walking in freedom and in fellowship with God. As soon as she believed the devil's lies, she was in bondage.

We know God has not changed, man has not changed, and neither has the devil. Jesus called the devil *"a liar and the father of lies"* (John 8:44). Satan appealed to Eve with self-centredness through lies; she accepted his lies as truth and lost her God-centredness. *We* are also tempted by the Enemy every day to believe and accept his lies as truth and to disregard or even disbelieve God's truth in certain areas of our lives. The moment we fall for this trick, we are defeated in that particular area. Paul declares that he is not ignorant of the devil's tactics (2 Corinthians 2:11), but if we are unaware of the strategy of the Enemy, we are defeated victims instead of *"more than conquerors"* (Romans 8:37).

God's call on my life for almost thirty years, I believe, has been to expose the lies of the Enemy in areas where a person is struggling and then help the individual to see the truth and be set free. To facilitate this approach, I teach how to identify both the motive and strategy of the Enemy, based on Scriptural accounts, as well as on personal experiences with people who have been set free. Many people, after I have given this teaching, have often asked, "Do you have this in writing? I won't be able to retain all this information." This book is an attempt to meet that need and also to reach more people.

I enjoy teaching and counseling, but "writing" is not my first love. Therefore, I have been impressed to write this book the way I teach. When I counsel people, I use many examples of real life situations that people can identify with. I have included many examples in this book but have changed the names of the counselees to protect their identities.

When I share with someone how to differentiate between the person's own thoughts and feelings and the thoughts and feelings imposed by the Enemy, I often see the person's eyes light up. When the truth hits him that many of the thoughts and feelings for which he has felt condemned or has even condemned himself for do not originate from him, he is filled with new hope and ambition to live the victorious life.

While it is exciting to witness a person begin to recognize and reject the lies of the Enemy, it is even more exciting to see the person grasp God's truth, which protects him from the lies. To know and agree with God's truth is our best protection against the Enemy, and it allows us to experience the "abundant life" because it releases God's power in our lives.

In the first part of this book, I concentrate on how to recognize the reality of the Enemy's tactics. Scripture passages clearly identify and attest the fact that the Enemy can and does work *in* people's lives and also works *through* people's lives, even though they are unaware of it. Jesus was very cognizant of the reality of the Enemy. The Bible records many incidents where Jesus dealt with him and set people free.

I am aware that some readers might get the impression that I am teaching "the devil made me do it." This is not true. The devil did not *make* Eve believe his lie, nor did he *make* her take the fruit and eat it, but he definitely *deceived* her into doing it. The same devil tempted Jesus after His forty day fast, but Jesus did not yield to the temptation as Eve did because He stood firmly on God's Word and said, *"It is written"* (Matthew 4:4,7,10). Because the devil succeeded in deceiving Eve, he had power over her. Since the devil was unable to deceive Jesus, he had no power over Him.

The second half of this book deals with the truths of God that we need to know in order to enable us to defeat the Enemy, even as Jesus did. If we know the unchangeable truths of God and choose to agree with them, we become invincible to the lies of the Enemy but become vessels for God to use for His glory.

James says,

Submit yourselves therefore to God. Resist the devil, and he will flee from you. Draw nigh to God, and He will draw nigh to you (James 4:7,8b).

When do we have to resist the devil? Whenever he comes with deception, we need to recognize the source and resist him. However, when he comes through people or circumstances which we cannot control, we need to submit and focus on God, and not on the devil.

God could have insulated us from the devil the moment we were saved, but He did not. God uses the devil as the pruning shears to prune the branches so they will bear much fruit. In John 15:1,2, Jesus declares His Father is the Gardener who prunes the branches. God does not ask us to produce fruit but to bear the fruit that He produces in our lives. God is looking for vessels, not pumps. As long as we believe we have to produce the fruit, we focus on "self" rather than on God. God uses the devil to expose our self-centredness and our nothingness. Jesus says in John 15:5b, *"without me ye can do nothing."* Jesus knows we can do nothing, but often, *we* do not. God allows the devil to defeat us so that we will come to recognize our total dependence on Him. Paul had learned this, and he declares this revelation in Galatians 2:20:

> *I am crucified with Christ: nevertheless I live; yet not I, but Christ liveth in me and the life which I now live in the flesh I live by the faith of the Son of God, who loved me, and gave himself for me.*

Christ wants to be our life, to live in us, and produce His fruit through us. The devil has deceived us into believing that now that we are Christians, we must work for God. The reason the devil wants us to work for God is so that he can defeat us, discourage us, and even get us to give up. However, God allows the devil to defeat us so that we get to the end of ourselves. Then He can reveal Himself to us as the all in all.

A vivid example of this is when Jesus gave Satan permission to sift Simon Peter. Jesus knew that Peter was desirous to work for Him, but He also knew that much of what Peter did was still "of the flesh" and not of the Spirit. In Luke 22:31,32, Jesus says,

Simon, Simon, behold, Satan hath desired to have you, that he may sift you as wheat: But I have prayed for thee, that thy faith fail not: and when thou art converted, strengthen thy brethren.

Here we can clearly see God's purpose in giving the devil permission to sift Peter. It was so that God could convert Peter from self-centredness and self-reliance to God-centredness and total dependence on God. After the sifting and converting were complete, Peter preached the first message and three thousand souls were saved. I am personally convinced that if God had not allowed Satan to sift him, Peter's perspective would not have changed. He would thus have preached in the flesh and, as a result, the three thousand souls would not have been saved. God's ways are definitely higher than our ways.

In the last chapter of the book "The Exchanged Life," I teach truths that I believe are life-changing. These truths from the book of Romans are key if we desire to allow God to live "His life" through us, instead of trying to live "our life" for God.

CHAPTER ONE

The Biblical Exposure of the Devil

THE BIBLE RECORDS INCIDENTS of behaviour in different people that were definitely inspired by the devil. From these accounts, it seems that, often, the person involved was unaware that the devil or a demon was working directly through him or her. The person felt justified in doing or saying what he or she did, yet the Bible clearly ascribes the action to the Enemy.

From the following accounts, we can clearly see that the Enemy uses different tactics with different people. As we look at these incidents, it will become clear that we should not be *"ignorant of the Enemy's devices"* (2 Corinthians. 2:11):

Be sober, be vigilant; because your adversary the devil, as a roaring lion, walketh about, seeking whom he may devour: Whom resist steadfast in the faith... (1 Peter 5:8,9a).

In Ephesians 6:11,12, Paul advises:

Put on the whole armor of God, that ye may be able to stand against the wiles of the devil. For we wrestle not against flesh and blood, but... against the rulers of the darkness of this world, against spiritual wickedness in high places.

Satan infuses thoughts into our mind, imposes feelings into our emotions, and invokes plans for actions.

Eve: Genesis 3:1-6

Now the serpent was more subtle than any beast of the field which the Lord God had made. And he said unto the woman, Yea, hath God said, Ye shall not eat of every tree of the garden? And the woman said unto the serpent, We may eat of the fruit of the trees of the garden: But of the fruit of the tree which is in the midst of the garden, God hath said, Ye shall not eat of it, neither shall ye touch it, lest ye die. And the serpent said unto the woman, Ye shall not surely die: For God doth know that in the day ye eat thereof, then your eyes shall be opened, and ye shall be as gods, knowing good and evil. And the woman saw that the tree was good for food, and that it was pleasant to the eyes, and a tree to be desired to make one wise, she took of the fruit thereof, and did eat, and gave also unto her husband with her; and he did eat.

Satan beguiled Eve to disobey God. He said, *"Yea hath God said, Ye shall not eat of every tree of the garden?"* He tried to get her to doubt God's wisdom and goodness. Then he contradicted God, saying, *"Ye shall not surely die."* Next, he accused God of withholding something good from them, *"For God doth know that in the day ye eat thereof, then your eyes shall be opened, and ye shall be as gods, knowing good and evil."*

David: 1 Chronicles 21:1

"And Satan stood up against Israel, and provoked David to number Israel." David did not know that Satan was behind him, prodding. He took for granted that this was his own idea and plan. In verse 7 of this same chapter, it says, *"And God was displeased with this thing; therefore he smote Israel."* The reason God was displeased was that David chose to depend upon the size of his army rather than upon God. What was the result? Verse 14 tells us, *"So the Lord sent pestilence upon Israel: and there fell of Israel seventy thousand men."* What a price—to be duped by Satan into evaluating problems through our natural understanding!

Job

The devil destroyed everything Job had, inflicted sickness upon him, accused him of sinning, and tried to discourage him through his wife. We will discuss Job further in a later chapter.

Peter: Mark 8:31-33

And he began to teach them, that the Son of man must suffer many things, and be rejected of the elders, and of the chief priests, and scribes, and be killed, and after three days rise again. And he spake that saying openly. And Peter took him and began to rebuke him. But when he had turned about and looked on his disciples, he rebuked Peter, saying, Get thee behind me, Satan: for thou savorest not the things that be of God, but the things that be of men.

Satan spoke through Peter to rebuke Jesus. Peter was unaware that it was Satan speaking through him; he thought this was his own thought, yet Jesus recognized where it came from and therefore said, *"Get thee behind me, Satan."*

Ananias and Sapphira: Acts 5:1-5

But a certain man named Ananias, with Sapphira his wife, sold a possession, and kept back part of the price, his wife also being privy to it, and brought a certain part, and laid it at the apostle's feet. But Peter said, Ananias, why hath Satan filled thine heart to lie to the Holy Ghost, and to keep back part of the price of the land? Whiles it remained, was it not thine own? and after it was sold, was it not in thine own power? why hast thou conceived this thing in thine heart? thou hast not lied unto men, but unto God. And Ananias hearing these words fell down, and gave up the ghost: and great fear came on all them that heard these things.

Satan provoked Ananias and Sapphira to pretend to be more spiritual than they were. In verse 3, Peter said, *"Ananias, why hath Satan filled thine heart to lie to the Holy Ghost, and keep back part of the price of the land?"* Satan tempted them to seek honour without paying the full price.

Jesus: Luke 4:1-13

And Jesus being full of the Holy Ghost returned from Jordan, and was led by the Spirit into the wilderness, Being forty days tempted of the devil. And in those days he did eat nothing: and when they were ended, he afterward hungered. And the devil said unto him, If thou be the Son of God, command this stone that it be made bread. And Jesus answered him, saying, It is written, That man shall not live by bread alone, but by every word of God. And the devil, taking him up into an high mountain, shewed unto him all the kingdoms of the world in a moment of time. And the devil said unto him, All this power will I give thee, and the glory of them: for that is delivered unto me; and to whomsoever I will I give it. If thou therefore wilt worship me, all shall be thine. And Jesus answered and said unto him, Get thee behind me, Satan: for it is written, Thou shalt worship the Lord thy God, and him only shalt thou serve. And he brought him to Jerusalem, and set him on a pinnacle of the temple, and said unto him, If thou be the Son of God, cast thyself down from hence: For it is written, He shall give his angels charge over thee, to keep thee: And in their hands they shall bear thee up, lest at any time thou dash thy foot against a stone. And Jesus answering said unto him, It is said, Thou shalt not tempt the Lord thy God. And when the devil had ended all the temptation, he departed from him for a season.

Satan attempted to dissuade Jesus from fulfilling God's purpose. He pretended to be sympathetic toward Jesus' physically weakened condition. He challenged Jesus to use God's power for His own purpose, to worship Satan or the things he stood for, and to tempt God to protect Him from harm, even though He would not be in God's will.

Paul: 2 Corinthians 12:7-10

And lest I should be exalted above measure through the abundance of the revelations, there was given to me a thorn in the flesh, the messenger of Satan to buffet me, lest I should be exalted above measure. For this thing I besought the Lord thrice, that it might depart from me. And he said unto me, My grace is sufficient for thee: for my strength is made perfect in weakness. Most gladly therefore will I rather glory in my infirmities, that the power of Christ may rest upon me. Therefore I take pleasure in infirmities, in reproaches, in necessities, in persecutions, in distresses for Christ's sake: for when I am weak, then am I strong.

It was the messenger of Satan that buffeted Paul.

Tares Among the Wheat: Matthew 13:38–39

The field is the world; the good seed are the children of the kingdom; but the tares are the children of the wicked one; The enemy that sowed them is the devil; the harvest is the end of the world; and the reapers are the angels.

The devil sowed tares among the good seed.

Stealing the Word: Mark 4:15

And these are they by the way side, where the word is sown; but when they have heard, Satan cometh immediately, and taketh away the word that was sown in their hearts.

The devil took the Word of God out of the hearts of those by the way side, so that they could not believe and be saved.

James and John: Luke 9:52-56

And Jesus sent messengers before his face: and they went, and entered into a village of the Samaritans, to make ready for him. And they did not receive him, because his face was as though he would go to

Jerusalem. And when his disciples James and John saw this, they said, Lord wilt thou that we command fire to come down from heaven, and consume them even as Elijah did? But he turned, and rebuked them, and said, Ye know not what manner of spirit ye are of. For the Son of man is not come to destroy men's lives, but to save them. And they went to another village.

The devil justified to James and John that the Samaritans, who rejected Jesus, should be destroyed by fire from Heaven. He got them to see this as "righteous anger," but Jesus declared in verse 55, *"Ye know not what manner of spirit ye are of."*

Saul and Judas: Luke 22:3-6; 1 Samuel 18:9-11

Then entered Satan into Judas surnamed Iscariot, being of the number of the twelve. And he went his way, and communed with the chief priests and captains, how he might betray him unto them. And they were glad, and covenanted to give him money. And he promised, and sought opportunity to betray him unto them in the absence of the multitude.

And Saul eyed David from that day and forward. And it came to pass on the morrow, that the evil spirit from God came upon Saul, and he prophesied in the midst of the house: and David played with his hand, as at other times: and there was a javelin in Saul's hand. And Saul cast the javelin; for he said, I will smite David even to the wall with it. And David avoided out of his presence twice.

The devil entered both Judas and Saul in order to kill.

The Gadarene Demoniac: Mark 5:1-5

And they came over unto the other side of the sea, into the country of the Gadarenes. And when he was come out of the ship, immediately there met him out of the tombs a man with an unclean spirit, Who had his dwelling among the tombs; and no man could bind him, no, not with chains: Because that he had been often bound with fetters and chains, and the chains had been plucked asunder by him, and the fetters broken in pieces: neither could any man tame him. And always, night and day, he was in the mountains, and in the tombs, crying, and cutting himself with stones.

It was a legion of demons that totally possessed the Gadarene demoniac. The demons preoccupied him with death *("Who had his dwelling among the tombs"),* they gave him supernatural powers (*"and no man could bind him, no, not with chains"*), and the demons imposed on him an overpowering urge to commit suicide *("crying, and cutting himself with stones").*

These examples from Scripture clearly indicate that the devil is out to kill, steal, and destroy. He uses the same tactics today. The more we are unaware of the wiles of the devil, the easier we make the devil's work.

CHAPTER TWO

Deliverance in the Ministry of Jesus

DURING THE TIME IN which the New Testament was written, people were very aware of demons and demonic activity. We read in the gospels how deliverance was such an essential part of Jesus' ministry, and how He addressed the demons with authority and commanded them to leave. Within Paul's writings, we also see this was a familiar subject to him and to the people of that time.

In a day and age in which the effects of demon activity are so vivid, surprisingly it is seldom discussed. We do not recognize that we are in a battle and that God has equipped us with the weapons to be victorious. The following study is designed to answer some basic questions about what the Bible says about demons and spiritual warfare.

There Is a Battle

For though we walk in the flesh, we do not war after the flesh: (For the weapons of our warfare are not carnal, but mighty through God to the pulling down of strongholds;) Casting down imaginations, and every high thing that exalteth itself against the knowledge of God, and bringing into captivity every thought to the obedience of Christ (2 Corinthians 10:3-5).

The thing that strikes us here is that we indeed are in a battle, a war that requires understanding of our Enemy, his tactics, his weapons, the battle ground, and the weapons that God has given to us to fight this battle and emerge victorious through Him: *"For the weapons of our warfare are not carnal, but mighty through God to the pulling down of strong holds."* Our weapons are not what we can do in the natural. Our tools cannot be anything other than what God has given to us, or otherwise, we will be ill-equipped. The Enemy is very strong. The word *stronghold* suggests a fortress, a well-fortified position. Only through God's power can we win against him.

When we have surrendered ground, we give the Enemy a beachhead in our lives, a fortified position from which he is able to wage further attack and offence.

Where is this battle taking place? According to the previous passage, it occurs in our thoughts and imaginations, *"bringing into captivity every thought to the obedience of Christ"* (2 Corinthians 10:5), literally subjecting our thoughts to scrutiny and seeing whether they stand before God as truth. We will explore the subject of thoughts in detail in chapters to come.

A warning is given to us in 2 Corinthians 2:11: *"Lest Satan get an advantage of us: for we are not ignorant of his devices."* In great clarity, Paul describes what we are up against. Sadly, most Christians are ignorant of the devices of the Enemy.

Israel has long been noted as having one of the most elite military units in the world. They accomplish successful mission after successful mission because they have mastered an amazing technique: before engaging in an offence operation, they first study their enemy. They gather intelligence and profiles about each sentry or officer that they might have to come up against. They know what weapons the enemy will have, where these weapons are located, and how their enemy might use each weapon. They will become so acquainted with their enemy, they will feel that they "know" him.

Our Enemy, the devil, studies and knows us. He knows exactly where our weaknesses are and how we react to situations, and, therefore, he often defeats us and puts us in bondage. If we are not aware of him and his tactics, then he has the advantage:

> *Put on the whole armour of God, that ye may be able to stand against the wiles of the devil.* [The wiles of the devil suggest the deceptive devices.] *For we wrestle not against flesh and blood, but against principalities, against powers, against the rulers of the darkness of this world, against spiritual wickedness in high places* (Ephesians 6:11,12).

We can see that the Enemy is deceptive by the fact that, in most cases, we aren't even aware that we are operating against an Enemy. We think that it is our own problem:

> *Above all, taking the shield of faith, wherewith ye shall be able to quench all the fiery darts of the wicked* (Ephesians 6:16).

In these two Scripture passages, Paul is making us aware that the Enemy is as real a foe today, as he was in the time of Jesus.

A Spirit of Infirmity: Can Sickness Be from Satan?

And, behold, there was a woman which had a spirit of infirmity eighteen years, and was bowed together, and could in no wise lift up herself. And when Jesus saw her, he called her to him, and said unto her, Woman, thou art loosed from thine infirmity And he laid his hands on her: and immediately she was made straight, and glorified God.... And ought not this woman, being a daughter of Abraham, whom Satan hath bound, lo, these eighteen years, be loosed from this bond on the Sabbath day? (Luke 13:11-13,16).

This is a clear indication that physical problems are often caused by spirits. But the physical sickness can be a symptom rather than the root cause. Dealing with only the external is like taking a painkiller when you have appendicitis. We would most likely see the woman's sickness in this passage as a physical problem, yet Jesus dealt with it as a spiritual problem.

One man I dealt with was a brilliant computer programmer, and he had been dramatically saved. When he was invited by another Christian to a Bible study, he panicked, knowing that at Bible studies, people often take turns reading. He believed he couldn't read because he knew only a sight vocabulary—if he was faced with a new word, he wouldn't be able to read it. He was afraid that people would find this out if he was forced to read out loud. This was the very thing that had driven him from Sunday school as a child. When I asked whether he had ever considered that his inability to read was just a lie, he said, "Of course not. I know I can't read new words." I said, "As a programmer you read technical languages, and it isn't sight vocabulary initially." He said, "I get it from context." Then I suggested to him that this was a demonic spirit hindering him, making him believe he couldn't read. We prayed and commanded that spirit to leave, and I handed him the open Bible, asking him to read. He read fluently. Shocked, he said, "If my wife heard this, she would fall out of her chair."

What seemed to be a mental disability was actually a spiritual problem. When we exposed the stronghold and dealt with the spiritual problem, this healed a mental interference. I believe that, often, our God-given abilities can be incapacitated by the Enemy's interference. This leaves us to wonder how much more we would succeed if we had no hindrances.

Silencing the Enemy

> *And devils also came out of many, crying out, and saying, Thou art Christ the Son of God. And he rebuking them suffered them not to speak: for they knew that he was Christ* (Luke 4:41).

> *And he healed many that were sick of divers diseases, and cast out many devils; and suffered not the devils to speak, because they knew him* (Mark 1:34).

It has puzzled many people that Jesus would silence the demons, especially when they were giving credence to Him and His position. Jesus silenced the demons because He knew that they would distort His ministry, adding lies to the truth. If they were allowed to speak, people would listen to both the truth and the lies, not knowing which was which.

We see this same idea in banks. When banks are training people to handle money, they initially allow them to come in contact only with real money so that when they come across counterfeit money, they will recognize it immediately.

Another example of this is found in the following Scripture passage:

And it came to pass, as we went to prayer, a certain damsel possessed with a spirit of divination met us, which brought her masters much gain by soothsaying; The same followed Paul and us, and cried, saying, These men are the servants of the most high God, which shew unto us the way of salvation. And this did she many days. But Paul, being grieved, turned and said to the spirit, I command thee in the name of Jesus Christ to come out of her. And he came out that same hour (Acts 16:16).

Why would the demons want to proclaim Jesus, except to distort the message? This has been a tactic that the devil has used since the beginning. When he deceived Eve, he distorted God's command to her, mixing truth with the lie.

The Full Gospel

*"The Spirit of the Lord is upon me, because he hath anointed me to preach the gospel to the poor; he hath sent me to heal the brokenhearted, to **preach deliverance** to the **captives**, and recovering of sight to the blind, to set at liberty them that are bruised, to preach the acceptable year of the Lord"* [emphasis mine] (Luke 4:18-19).

This is the first sermon that Jesus gave. According to Luke 4:18-19, the full gospel and ministry of Jesus was to preach the gospel, heal the broken-hearted, set the captives free, and to set

at liberty those who were bruised. The setting free of the captives—spiritual captives—was a daily part of His ministry and
still is an integral part of the ministry of the gospel today.

If Jesus never had cast out those demons, then those people would have never been free. Jesus wants Christians to be
free, and *"If the Son therefore shall make you free, ye shall be
free indeed"* (John 8:36). If we are not set free, then we are
not fully entering into God's will for our lives.

If You Believe

*And when he came to his disciples, he saw a great
multitude about them, and the scribes questioning with
them. And straightway all the people, when they
beheld him, were greatly amazed, and running to him
saluted him. And he asked the scribes, What question
ye with them? And one of the multitude answered and
said, Master, I have brought unto thee my son, which
hath a dumb spirit; And wheresoever he taketh him, he
teareth him: and he foameth, and gnasheth with his
teeth, and pineth away: and I spake to thy disciples
that they should cast him out; and they could not. He
answereth him, and saith, O faithless generation, how
long shall I be with you? how long shall I suffer you?
bring him unto me. And they brought him unto him:
and when he saw him, straightway the spirit tare him;
and he fell on the ground, and wallowed foaming. And
he asked his father, How long is it ago since this came
unto him? And he said, Of a child. And ofttimes it hath
cast him into the fire, and into the waters, to destroy
him: but if thou canst do any thing, have compassion
on us, and help us. Jesus said unto him, If thou canst*

31

believe, all things are possible to him that believeth. And straightway the father of the child cried out, and said with tears, Lord, I believe; help thou mine unbelief. When Jesus saw that the people came running together, he rebuked the foul spirit, saying unto him, Thou dumb and deaf spirit, I charge thee, come out of him, and enter no more into him. And the spirit cried, and rent him sore, and came out of him: and he was as one dead; insomuch that many said, He is dead. But Jesus took him by the hand, and lifted him up; and he arose. And when he was come into the house, his disciples asked him privately, Why could not we cast him out? And he said unto them, This kind can come forth by nothing, but by prayer and fasting (Mark 9:14-29).

Though Jesus had not died as yet and caused the devil's final defeat, He had already defeated demons in His life on a daily basis. Jesus told the disciples the reason they had not been able to cast the demon out was because of their unbelief. Whenever Jesus uses the word "unbelief" or the phrase "you of little faith," what He is really saying is that we are not applying our faith to the given situation.

Jesus expects us to believe not only in the reality of demons, but also that God wants to set us free from them. He does not want us to co-exist with them or be fooled into believing that they are part of us. *"If thou canst believe, all things are possible to him that believeth."* What a statement! Jesus says that if you can believe, then it is possible. The father of the boy answered, *"and said with tears, Lord, I believe; help thou mine unbelief."* What an incredible step of faith! I believe what he was saying was, "Lord, I choose to believe, give me the faith that I lack!"

If we have a hard time believing the reality of demons in everyday life, or if we struggle in believing that we can walk in victory and be more than conquerors, then we need to say as this father did, *"Lord, I believe; help thou mine unbelief."* This belief is a choice—a choice to believe that what the Bible says is true.

What New Doctrine Is This?

> *And there was in their synagogue a man with an unclean spirit; and he cried out, Saying, Let us alone; what have we to do with thee, thou Jesus of Nazareth? art thou come to destroy us? I know thee who thou art, the Holy One of God. And Jesus rebuked him, saying, Hold thy peace, and come out of him. And when the unclean spirit had torn him, and cried with a loud voice, he came out of him. And they were all amazed, insomuch that they questioned among themselves, saying, What thing is this? what new doctrine is this? for with authority commandeth he even the unclean spirits, and they do obey him. And immediately his fame spread abroad throughout all the region round about Galilee* (Mark 1:23-28).

After Jesus had cast out the unclean spirit, the people witnessing it were so amazed they questioned among themselves, saying,

> *What thing is this? what new doctrine is this? for with authority commandeth he even the unclean spirits, and they do obey him* (Mark 1:27).

Though they were aware of the problem, it was the authority Jesus had to deal with the problem which amazed them.

On one hand, we are often aware, at least intellectually, that Jesus is the solution to our problems, but often we are not aware of the problem of demons. Thus, you may find yourself asking, just as the people in Jesus time did, "What new doctrine is this?" I can tell you, I am not teaching new doctrine, but because many haven't been taught how the Enemy works and how to be set free, it seems new. Jesus told us in Mark 16:17, *"And these signs shall follow them that believe; In my name shall they cast out devils."* This was Jesus' last commission or commandment to us before His ascension. This really isn't a new doctrine, just a neglected one, and if we don't obey, we are actually sinning against Him.

The Gadarene Demoniac

In Mark 5:1-20, we have the story of the Gadarene demoniac who was so preoccupied with death, he made his dwelling among the tombs! The first lady I counseled in deliverance had a similar preoccupations with death. In her district, they did not bury the dead in wintertime, but stored them in the funeral home in their caskets. She would go in that room and talk to the people in the caskets. Also, the first thing that she looked for in a newspaper was the obituary section—she was obsessed with death and suicide.

The Gadarene demoniac's dwelling was among the tombs: *"and no man could bind him, no, not with chains"* (vs. 3). He also had supernatural strength and power: *"the chains had been plucked asunder by him, and the fetters broken in pieces: neither could any man tame him, nobody could subdue him, or control him"* (vs. 4). This shows the tremendous physical power that demons can exercise through a person. Often we think that, "My problem is just me, and I am really messed up," but if the devil could do that, then couldn't he do similar things today to handicap us or to interfere in our lives?

By getting us to believe in mental illness, the devil has made a cover for himself beneath which he can work. This gives people an alibi not to do anything, and they suffer as a result. Jesus says to the Christian, *"You are more than conquerors"* (Romans 8:37). I believe that we need to examine nervous breakdowns. I challenge any doctor to show me the nerve that broke down. Rather than taking for granted that "nerves" are messed up, we should prayerfully check out whether it isn't demons. They are so subtle, and we are so ignorant in this area. We like to call them "inabilities," "overloads," or "breakdowns," but the Enemy can cause them all, and he often does.

This Gadarene demoniac was totally dysfunctional: *"And always, night and day, he was in the mountains, and in the tombs, crying, and cutting himself with stones"* (vs. 5), yet, when he was delivered, the change was instant and profound. Underneath the horrible oppression, he was a completely normal person. Could there be things in your life that may be hindered by demons as well?

Demons Have Names and Positions

Mark 5 shows that demons even have names. In this incident in Mark, Jesus asked,

What is thy name? And he [the demon] *answered, saying, **My** name is Legion: for **we** are many* [emphasis mine] (Mark 5:9).

Obviously, this was a demon with rank and with jurisdiction. Demons not only have names, but their names often reveal their function. It is often important to identify a demon's name because we then can get to the root of the problem. When they have to expose their name(s), some of their power is also taken away. As long as we don't know their name, we don't understand their function and may interpret it as the person himself. **The demon's strength lies in their ability to remain hidden**. If we don't recognize the demon behind the problem, we may believe that it is ourselves or something else that is hindering, thus enabling the demons to carry on unhindered. The moment we believe the devil's lies, we give him power, as did Eve in the Garden of Eden.

Binding the Strongman

But if I cast out devils by the Spirit of God, then the kingdom of God is come unto you. Or else how can one enter into a strong man's house, and spoil his goods, except he first bind the strong man? and then he will spoil his house (Matthew 12:28-29).

Jesus said that we have to bind the strongman first. This would imply a demon of authority, for if we only cast out some lesser demons, the strongman remains and is able to continue his work.

Then said he unto me, Fear not, Daniel: for from the first day that thou didst set thine heart to understand, and to chasten thyself before thy God, thy words were heard, and I am come for thy words. But the prince of the kingdom of Persia withstood me one and twenty days: but, lo, Michael, one of the chief princes, came to help me; and I remained there with the kings of Persia (Daniel 10:12–13).

Here we see a battle that is raging in the spiritual realm, between a demon called, "The Prince of Persia" and the angel Michael. "The Prince over Persia" likely had many lower demons to help him hinder the answer from coming to Daniel. This might be why we often don't get immediate answers to prayer.

Don't Mock the Devil

Many Christians who recognize the reality of demons will command them to go to Hell. Jesus did not cast demons into Hell, but simply commanded them to go. Now, if there were enough demons in one man to make two thousand pigs go crazy, wouldn't it have been better to just get rid of them altogether? If we could do that, we could cast all demons into Hell and have a demon roundup and solve the problem entirely. However, this is not what Jesus commands us to do. Remember, the tools we use cannot be anything other than what God has given to us. If we go beyond God's commands, we can't effectively fight the Enemy. The Enemy is strong enough that only through God's power can we win against him:

> *Yet Michael the archangel, when contending with the devil he disputed about the body of Moses, durst not bring against him a railing accusation, but said, The Lord rebuke thee* (Jude 1:9).

We must not mock the devil, though we need to be confident, not in ourselves, but in the power of Jesus and in the fact that He has already conquered the Enemy. We can walk in the same victory.

Why Are You Afraid?

> *And they come to Jesus, and see him that was possessed with the devil, and had the legion, sitting, and clothed, and in his right mind: and they were afraid* (Mark 5:15).

37

Why would they be afraid? Most people do not want to hear about demons because it makes them uncomfortable.

And they that saw it told them how it befell to him that was possessed with the devil, and also concerning the swine. And they began to pray him to depart out of their coasts (Mark 5:16,17).

Here we see an interesting contrast of responses to Jesus' deliverance ministry. In the story of the young man being delivered, it was said that the people marvelled, and Jesus' fame spread abroad. The people were thankful that Jesus could set people free. But here in this story of the Gadarene demoniac, they wanted to get rid of Jesus.

Does it bother us that Jesus set people free and desires to do so today? It surely shouldn't! If it does, perhaps it is not our own thoughts that trouble us, but resistance from the Enemy, wanting to protect himself.

And when Simon saw that through laying on of the apostles' hands the Holy Spirit was given, he offered them money, saying, Give me also this power, that whomsoever I lay hands, he may receive the Holy Ghost. But Peter said unto him, Thy money perish with thee, because thou hast thought that the gift of God may be purchased with money (Acts 8:18-20).

The devil often uses extremes. Either he wants us to reject the knowledge of demons and deliverance from them, or he wants us to have an abnormal fascination and be involved for selfish reasons. The people who saw the Gadarene Demoniac set free rejected Jesus, whereas Simon's yearning for spiritual power in Acts 8 was selfishly motivated. Both of these types of responses are governed by the devil. They show the devil's scope of strategy. By the devil blinding us to the reality of demons, he robs us of the tremendous deliverance and victory available to us. Because of this, our walk as Christians does not impact many people.

Search the Scriptures

These were more noble than those in Thessalonica, in that they received the word with all readiness of mind, and searched the scriptures daily, whether those things were so (Acts 17:11).

We are told to search the Scriptures, not so much to discredit its teaching, but to find the truth. The motives behind our searching the Scriptures makes all the difference:

Study to show thyself approved unto God, a workman that needeth not to be ashamed, rightly dividing the word of truth (2 Timothy 2:15).

Whom the Son Sets Free

And when he [Jesus] *was come into the ship, he that had been possessed with the devil* [the Gadarene demoniac] *prayed him that he might be with him. Howbeit Jesus suffered him not, but saith unto him, Go home to thy friends, and tell them how great things the Lord hath done for thee, and hath had compassion on thee. And he departed, and began to publish in Decapolis how great things Jesus had done for him: and all men did marvel* (Mark 5:18-20).

The Gadarene was now an effective witness. In the same way, deliverance frees us to be a vessel and a witness for God. God could have invented the tape recorder six thousand years ago and pumped us full of the gospel, but instead, He used (and still uses) witnesses who had experienced the love of God. The Gadarene had experienced this love, and from what is written, it would seem that he became very devoted to Jesus. If we relegate the devil as only a force or even just a concept, as some do, we will not experience the abundant life that Jesus came to give.

CHAPTER THREE

How I Began

The Spirit of the Lord is upon me, because he hath anointed me to preach the gospel to the poor; he hath sent me to heal the brokenhearted, to preach deliverance to the captives, and recovering of sight to the blind, to set at liberty them that are bruised, To preach the acceptable year of the Lord (Luke 4:18).

MANY CHURCHES *"preach the gospel to the poor,"* but sadly, that is where they stop. The ministry of Jesus consisted of much more, and our ministry ought to reflect His.

When I teach, whether at Living Faith Bible College, in churches, or during summer camps, I survey the masked faces before me. They all appear to be on top of things. They raise their hands to God in worship, they sing His praises, but when they come into my office, often broken hearts and defeated lives surface. We are living in an age where we have been trained to put on a front to protect ourselves. We are convinced that people will think less of us if they know what is going on inside of us. Consequently, we hide the hurt and confusion behind intricate facades. We need healing and deliverance; we need to see truth and be set free.

Some of the things I will be sharing are going to be new and radical, and I urge you, that rather than rejecting anything outright, put the concept on a shelf for a time and look at it later when you may have need of it. You might find it makes more sense as applicable situations arise.

Superior Battle Technique

When explorers came to the Americas three centuries ago, they came into lands already inhabited by aboriginal peoples. Often, tension arose between them, sometimes turning into all-out war. The explorers, without understanding their enemy, would don their bright uniforms, beat their drums, and march in straight columns into battle. The aboriginal people took great advantage of this ignorance and would hide themselves in the woods and silently take out one bright target after the other, inflicting great loss on the bewildered explorers. Although the explorers had superior weapons and firepower, the aboriginal people had superior technique and strategy.

We, as Christians, are in a battle, and often we do not know the techniques of our Enemy the devil and his demons. Consequently, we are often taken by surprise. Worse, still, we do not recognize that we are in the battle and, thus, end up whipping ourselves because we fail to recognize the Enemy.

To illustrate, it wasn't until the turn of the last century that medicine fully grasped the menace of bacteria. More people died in surgery than those who survived. After examining a dead body, a doctor would not think twice about delivering a baby without ever washing his hands. People were entirely ignorant of the existence of bacteria, and many deaths were caused because of this ignorance. But one day, as Doctor Leeuwenhoek suspiciously viewed a sample of soil beneath the lens of his microscope, he saw what his eye alone could not see and exclaimed, "The ground is alive!" Indeed, it was, and this was to be one of the most revolutionary discoveries ever made in the realm of modern medicine. Today, it would be unthinkable to neglect the sterilization and cleanliness that has become such a standard part of medicine. In the same way, we need that same microscope in our lives, showing us what we cannot visibly see.

The same is seen when a person has a tumour on his brain. He will not likely be aware of the tumour at first, but eventually he will begin to suffer. Motor skills will be impaired, and he may be subject to violent or irrational behaviour. Seeing this strange behaviour, others might be tempted to believe that the person is crazy, and the person may believe it too! However, when the doctor discovers the tumour, determines whether it is malignant or not, and has it removed, there is relief in knowing "why." Ignorance is no longer a bondage.

A Reluctant Beginning

Although I was a Bible school graduate, I knew very little about how the devil worked. I knew that Jesus dealt with demons and that missionaries talked about them, but I didn't know we had them here in Canada.

In 1973, during the time that I was employed as a high school counselor, a number of adults came for counseling.

One lady that came to see me was an attractive twenty-nine year old who had been a Christian for seventeen years. Her name was Grace. She was hurting deeply, but had learned to cover up in front of people. Name any problem and she had it.

As Grace shared with me, I began to notice that the theories I had learned in university did not fit. She would say that she never loved her husband, never wanted to love him, and didn't care if he became a Christian or not. However, later in our discussion Grace would contradict herself and would indicate that the opposite was true. When I pointed out this inconsistency, her eyes glazed over and she exclaimed, "I hate you! I could hit you!" Shocked at her own behaviour, moments later she would say, "Whatever, made me say that? That is not the way I feel at all!"

This convinced me that there was something else speaking and reacting through her, yet, I was not equipped to deal with it. I asked her if we could meet again, thus allowing me the chance to seek God about her problems.

At that time, I had heard that there had been a ministers' conference on spiritual warfare at the Bible school I graduated from. I decided to find out more about this spiritual warfare and drove 200 miles to talk to the president of the Bible school. I shared with him the problems that Grace was having, and he agreed with my suspicion that it was probably demonic. He shared the things he had learned from dealing with people since he received training from the conference. He gave me a tape of some of the teachings and encouraged me to step out in faith and to try to help bring deliverance to Grace.

I went home and listened to the tape several times over with a friend of mine. On this tape there were recordings of several counseling sessions, and we actually heard demons speak through the counselees—often in different voices—even a man's voice speaking through a lady and vice versa.

I began to see that this was real. I saw that demons hadn't changed since Christ died, and people hadn't changed either.

If the devil worked through people back then, why wouldn't he work through them now?

After my friend and I had listened to the tapes several times, we discussed them, comparing them with Scripture. I went through the Gospels and was surprised at how many times Jesus addressed demons. He understood the problem and then addressed them accordingly. We decided to step out in faith.

I was somewhat reluctant to set out on this yet largely unknown course. I certainly didn't want to get into a situation that could make things worse, for there is a Scriptural caution that says,

> *When the unclean spirit is gone out of a man, he walketh through the dry places, seeking rest; and finding none, he saith, I will return unto my house whence I came out. And when cometh, he findeth it swept and garnished. Then goeth he and taketh to him seven other spirits more wicked than himself; and they enter in, and dwell there: and the last state of that man is worse than the first* (Luke 11:24-26).

With this serious possibility in mind, my friend (who was a fellow teacher) and I decided that it would be wise to work together on this.

We met with Grace again and explained to her what we had learned and concluded. It made sense to her, so we chose to meet together on the following Monday.

In the week before she was to come, Grace's body became riddled with pain. She went to her doctor, and he wanted to hospitalize her. Grace decided not to go to the hospital until she had the chance to be delivered from demons on Monday. When she arrived at my office, she lowered herself slowly into the chair, and then my friend and I proceeded the way we heard it done. We commanded the demon that was afflicting her with pain to come to attention. This was a real case of stepping out in faith for the both of us.

I can't remember how many times we commanded, but nothing seemed to happen. All of a sudden, a demon took over. I'm sure my hair stood on end! I have seen angry people before, but when a demon looks at you through the eyes of a person, those eyes are evil! Grace violently lunged at me. I was so taken by surprise because, even though I had heard this kind of thing on the tapes, I wasn't prepared for this! My faith was so small at that moment, but praise God, my faith was in the right person! I commanded the demon in her saying, "In the name of Jesus, SIT DOWN!" Grace just fell back in the chair. When I saw what impact this had on the demon, my faith really increased.

I commanded the demons to give their names in accordance with how Jesus commanded demons. We got the names of seven. As we commanded these demons one by one to go in the Name of Jesus, guttural sounds came out of her from deep within her body. She looked like she would throw up and fell to the floor.

When these seven demons had departed, Grace's eyes were clear. She had been totally oblivious to the events of the previous two hours. The last thing she remembered was lowering herself into the chair in agony. Her first comment was, "What about the pain? It's gone!" She then literally hopped about the room free from the awful pain she had first come with.

Grace continued to come for counseling as there were other demons from which she needed deliverance. This is similar to an iceberg. We can see the obvious problem, but a problem ten times its magnitude lurks beneath the surface. As we begin to break away what is on the surface, more ice will rise to the surface. This often is the case in deliverance; once we have exposed and removed one set of demons, another set is exposed and can then be dealt with.

One day as we were talking, I noticed Grace fingering the broach she was wearing. As we began talking about it, she said, "This *is* my mother's broach!," I noticed her emphasis on the word "is." I questioned her, "Is?" knowing that her mother had already passed away some time ago. Grace looked puzzled for a few moments and then said strongly, "*Is!* Although I know my mother died, to me she is still alive. She is still telling me how to hang the pillow cases on the clothes-line." Grace began to tell me how her relationship with her mother had always been dysfunctional. All throughout her life, Grace's mother had nagged her about everything, and when she died, the demon that had attacked her through her mother apparently transferred to her. That is why it seemed like her mother was still talking. After recognizing that this was a demon, I commanded him to leave in the Name of Jesus, and he did.

Another demon we came across was named "Complete Destruction." When I commanded him, he sneered, "I own her and have possessed her before she was born!" Grace had been very suicidal. She told me that whenever she came to the railroad track, she had an intense urge to drive the car in front of the train or right into the side of it. It took everything in her to bring the car to a stop.

We commanded "Complete Destruction" to leave on three separate occasions, and yet nothing happened. On the fourth attempt he sneered, "You have tried four times to get me out, and you have not been able to." I searched my heart for unconfessed sin in my life but could not pinpoint any. It was a little later that Grace telephoned me, "I cannot confess this certain sin because 'Complete Destruction' presented himself to me and told me if I confessed, he would kill me!" She was gripped with fear, and I was powerless to help her until she confessed.

A few days later, Grace called me again in terrible physical agony. She requested that we meet. When my friend and I walked into the room, the demon manifested. I recognized it by now. I had seen this same demon four times before. It sneered at me and said, "You are not going to get me out!" I didn't know what to do.

Then "Complete Destruction" attacked her physically. My partner and I felt led by the Holy Spirit not to interfere. Grace began to convulse, the demon was literally throwing her around, and it was terrible to witness. We waited for a minute or so before commanding him, but it seemed like a very long minute. We commanded "Complete Destruction" to release her, and she relaxed.

Then she said, "I am going to confess that sin. I lied to you about a certain sin in my life."

The moment she confessed her lie, she had a release, and when I commanded "Complete Destruction" to go, his reaction reminded me of a dog with its tail between its legs. He couldn't even put up a resistance. This showed that it was the unconfessed sin that had given the Enemy power.

When Grace first came to see me, she would say, "I have felt unwanted since my mother's womb." I thought that all she meant was, "...as long as I can remember." But I was really amazed when she insisted, "I really can remember being in my mother's womb!" I thought it weird, but it wasn't until several years later that I understood what this meant.

Reincarnated?

I was asked to counsel a man named Boris, who had come from Eastern Europe after World War II. He was an intelligent man, an architect, and he claimed to be a Christian. Boris had a number of problems and had undergone some unusual experiences. He began to speak about his belief in reincarnation. I challenged his belief in reincarnation. His answer was, "It has to be!" Then he began to relate how after he had arrived in Canada, before he would enter an unfamiliar home, he knew what picture hung on which wall, how the furniture was arranged, and the structural layout, as if he had been there before. This foreknowledge convinced him that he must have had a previous life. Boris had never lived a previous life, but it was a demon that knew about the homes and communicated this knowledge to him in such a way that it seemed to to be his own knowledge.

All of a sudden, a light went on within my spirit. I put the cases of Grace and Boris together. How could Grace remember being in her mother's womb? The demon that entered her in her mother's womb had the knowledge and had imposed this awareness on Grace. The demon would bring to her remembrance of its awareness, and Grace thought that it was her own memory.

Staying Free

Then Jesus said to those Jews which believed on him, If ye continue in my word, then you are my disciples indeed; And ye shall know the truth and the truth shall make you free (John 8:31–32).

God was so gracious in that first case with Grace. He gave us total success. We would command a demon to leave in the Name of Jesus, and he would leave. This did much to build my faith. God knew how little I really knew and yet He used me and great things resulted.

Initially, I thought I had found the answer to every man's problem! However, as time went on, I discovered the importance of sound teaching as part of the deliverance. When a demon left, there was a dramatic change, but if the person didn't understand what gave the Enemy the stronghold in the first place, he might still believe the same lies that gave the Enemy the power to begin with. Those who were delivered needed the understanding to keep the demons out from then on.

I discovered that I needed to help people identify the lies and the truth. Initially I would teach after deliverance, but now I teach beforehand. If I can help show people what are lies and what God's truth is, then they have the tools to remain in victory.

———— CHAPTER FOUR ————

Exposing the Enemy

◆

PAUL SAID, "I AM not ignorant of the devices of the enemy" (2 Corinthians 2:11). Most Christians, though, *are* unaware of his tactics.

I have discovered that deliverance is 90 percent teaching. There is no doubt that in my early days of doing deliverance, people were set free from demonic spirits. Suicidal people were set free and the urge to kill themselves was gone. However, they did not necessarily walk in total victory for any length of time, and that made me uneasy. If a person continues to believe the lies that the devil feeds him, although the demon may have been cast out, it gives the Enemy power in his life. Since then, my approach has changed. I now help people to identify the lies that they believe, and what the truth is in that area. This makes it easier to get rid of the spirits, and then they walk in complete victory. Many times when the person grasps the truth and renounces the lies, the demons just leave without having to be cast out, which will later be illustrated by the testimony of Michael, who was struggling with homosexuality.

In my first deliverance session, after we got rid of the initial set of demons, I was thrilled. I could identify with the seventy disciples when they came back and said, "Even the demons obey us." I experienced their excitement because when those demons were lunging at me, and I commanded them to sit, they would fall back into the seat. When I commanded them to leave, they had to leave. It is exciting when demons have to obey you, but it is even more exciting when I see people walking in the truth. Then we don't have to deal in deliverance. As we learn to identify the devices of the Enemy, and as we learn the ways of God and apply these things, we will walk in the victory God intends for each one of us.

Remaining Hidden

Kim had gone for counseling and to psychiatrists for years, yet the demons never manifested. However, the demon recognized that I knew that a demon was behind the problem, and there was no value for it to remain in hiding and therefore it manifested in great violence. At one point, as her husband and I were pinning Kim down, the demon said, "She should go to a psychiatrist and he would lock her up." If Kim had reacted in the psychiatrist's office the way she did in mine, she would certainly have been locked up. That was the intent of this demon: to get her locked up and, ultimately, to destroy her.

Misconceptions

Some people believe that Christians cannot have demons living in them. The Bible says we are the temple of the Holy Spirit. The temple in the Old Testament had the outer court, the inner court, and the Holy of Holies. Consider the outer court as being the body, the soul being the inner court, and the spirit being the Holy of Holies.

Everybody had access to the outer court, which meant sin could enter because people had sin. The inner court (the Holy place), was where the priests offered the daily sacrifices, but they still had sin in their lives. However, nobody with sin could enter the Holy of Holies because the presence of God dwelt there. If a Priest entered the Holy of Holies with sin in his life, he was struck dead.

The Holy Spirit lives in our spirit as Christians and, therefore, the presence of God is in our spirit. That makes it impossible for an evil spirit to enter a Christian's spirit. I belong to God, therefore, I cannot become demon-possessed, only oppressed. (Ownership belongs to God.)

The devil can affect my body and soul. We know that Jesus healed the sick and that sometimes when He cast out a demon, the sickness would leave as well. So, we know that demons can definitely affect our body. I come across this all the time.

The first lady I counseled would say, "Oh, I am so sick, I am going to vomit!" At first, I would let her go out and use the washroom, but nothing would happen. Then I caught onto the devil's trick. It was a demon who made her feel sick in order to get her out of the room because he did not want to be cast out.

Demons can definitely affect our body, and through our thoughts and feelings, they can affect our outward life. Sadly, many Christians are, to a lesser or greater degree, robots of the Enemy because he has programmed their beliefs. Often this influence begins in childhood when a lie is first accepted. The devil implants a lie, and once it is believed as truth, he does not have to do much because people will continue telling the lie to themselves. The devil just has to make sure that it stays alive.

Fear and Low Self-Esteem

Annette came to me plagued with many fears. She was afraid to make a telephone call, go into a restaurant, or go into water. She wanted to be set free from the fears. All of her life, Annette had believed that she was fat and ugly. The Enemy used many situations in her childhood to reinforce this belief.

Annette's mother had exposed her to the occult by inviting a poltergeist into their home. The poltergeist made the blinds open and shut on their own accord, the TV would go on and off, and sometimes items would disappear for no apparent reason and then return an hour later. This provided an opening through which the Enemy gained a foothold in Annette's life.

When Annette's mother would become abusive towards her, Annette would go out to the barn to work with her dad. Because Annette often worked in the barn before going to school, she would not have time to wash up. On the school bus, the other children, including her brothers and sisters, refused to sit with her because they said she stank. These experiences did nothing to improve her self-image.

No matter how much Annette's husband and others told her how beautiful she was, she was unable to believe them because she would look into the mirror and see herself as fat and ugly. I had her say aloud the verse, *"I am fearfully and wonderfully made"* (Psalm 139:14) while looking into the mirror. When Annette first began to quote this Scripture, it was difficult; it went against everything that she felt and thought about herself. When she was able to see the lie and how ridiculous it was, there was a breakthrough and she was set free. She began to see and verbalize the truth. The Bible says, *"Confess with your mouth and believe in your heart"* [emphasis mine] (Romans 10:9). Choosing to confess often comes before we really believe it. When we confess the **lies** that the Enemy feeds us about ourselves, we begin to believe them and then act accordingly. When Annette began confessing what the Bible said about her, which was truth, she started to believe it and was set free.

Sold to the Devil

One year, a woman named Laura was brought to our camp. Her friends didn't know what to do with her, and she didn't know what to do with herself. When talking with her, I realized that Laura was by far the worst case I had ever had. Both her mother and grandmother were witches. As a child Laura had been sold to the devil. Satanists had taken her pet dog, the only living thing that she could relate to, and cut off its head and sprinkled its blood over her, and dedicated her to the devil. As a small child Laura had witnessed a human sacrifice. Needless to say, this girl was in great bondage.

Laura was twenty-three years old, a little chubby, and about five feet tall. She had a poor self-image and always saw herself as ugly. After dealing with one particular demon, she said she felt a sensation on her hands. She looked at her hands and saw that the wrinkles she had always perceived had disappeared. Laura exclaimed, "I don't have wrinkles any more!" This particular demon had given her the perception that she had wrinkles that she alone could see. Now she was free. This is similar to how an anorexic sees nothing but fat, when it is in fact the farthest thing from the truth.

There are two ways of getting rid of demons. One is to cast them out; the other is to starve them out. People who have had demons cast out must learn how to walk in victory. The ones who starve them out learn what lies give the demon a right. They isolate the lie, ask forgiveness for believing the lie, and speak the truth. Then the demon really has no choice but to leave, and the person can walk in victory. People who starve demons out also know how to keep them out, whereas people that have them cast out have not necessarily learned to walk in victory. It doesn't matter to me which way the demons leave, as long as they leave.

The devil likes to remain hidden, but when he is exposed, he will try to consume a person's focus so that the person concentrates on fighting the devil—constantly engaging him—when really the person should recognize him, but focus his attention on God.

For example, if a girl has a boyfriend and another fellow becomes interested in her, she has two ways that she can deal with him. She could say, "I don't want anything to do with you" whenever he comes around. However, since she is talking to him, he may not believe her because she is still showing him a form of attention. A more effective way would be to ignore this second fellow and pay all the attention to the first fellow. The second fellow would soon get the message. This same method works on the devil. I would much rather focus on things of God and on His power than on the Enemy.

Demons are disembodied spirits. I am not concerned about whether the demon is in my body, or if he sits on my shoulder, or walks behind me and tells me lies. The effect is the same. The devil would like us to become embarrassed and therefore unable to admit we have a demonic problem, especially if the demon is living in our body. It really doesn't matter if it is inside or outside, the problem is still the same. For example, I don't think that Peter had a demon living inside him, but the demon influenced both his thoughts and feelings. Much of demon activity is imposed on us from the outside, but there are times when the demon is inside a person's body. It usually enters through some traumatic experience or exposure to things of the occult, and demons that have entered before birth are very difficult to deal with.

Differing Levels of Manifestation

Having worked twenty-seven years in deliverance, I have noticed three differing levels of manifestations of demons.

The most common level of manifestation of demons is where the person acts totally normal, but during counseling, they will have thoughts or feelings imposed on them that makes it apparent that a demon is present. In this case, you really need the person's immediate cooperation to share the thoughts they do not choose to think themselves. This helps the person to recognize what they are up against, and it enables me, as the counselor, to help identify the demon for them.

In the second level of manifestation, a demon uses the person's vocal cords and speaks out loud, or even uses the person to try to attack the counselor. The demon takes over the person's faculties, yet the person will remain lucid and aware of what is happening, though they are powerless to stop it.

In the third level of manifestation, the demon takes over the person's consciousness, and as a result, the person is completely unaware of what is happening. As the counselor, you deal directly with the demon, and the person has no active part whatsoever. Remember the example of Grace. The last thing she remembered was lowering herself into the chair in pain, and then two hours later when she regained her consciousness, her first awareness was the absence of pain. She had no recollection of what occurred, although many demons had departed. I had to share with her what had happened. This is the most extreme level of manifestation and is somewhat rare.

I believe that the Lord early on gave me knowledge of the many ways the Enemy can be involved and of the tactics he uses so that I would understand the scope of the Enemy's functioning. The Enemy doesn't need new tricks because we still fall for the old ones. I trust that these examples will facilitate understanding of how often the roots of our problems are caused by the Enemy and how we can be freed.

Although I have shared these incidents concerning demons, I don't want people to become afraid or to focus too much on the demons. The purpose is to clearly show that we are in a battle, so that we may understand and focus on God's truth.

CHAPTER FIVE

Body, Soul, and Spirit

IN THOSE EARLY YEARS of counseling, I developed a diagram to help people understand and differentiate between how the Enemy affects humans and interferes in our lives, in contrast to how God works in our lives.

> *And the very God of peace sanctify you wholly; and I pray God your whole **spirit** and **soul** and **body** be preserved blameless unto the coming of our Lord Jesus Christ* [emphasis mine] (Thessalonians 5:23).

> *For the word of God is quick, and powerful, and sharper than any two-edged sword, piercing even to the dividing asunder of **soul** and **spirit**, and of the joints and marrow[**body**], and is a discerner of the thoughts and intents of the heart* [emphasis mine] (Hebrews 4:12).

From these two Scripture passages, we see that man is a tri-unity, made up of body, soul, and spirit.

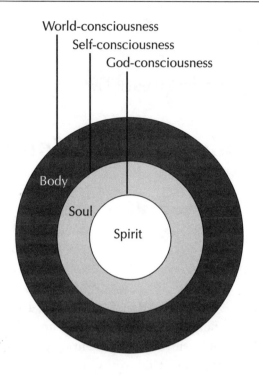

Figure 5.1 - Man: A Triune Being

THE BODY is our world-consciousness. Through the five senses, we are aware of what goes on around us. This is the physiological aspect.

THE SOUL can be defined as our self-consciousness, the awareness of who we are and how we relate to other people. This is the psychological aspect.

THE SPIRIT, is our God-consciousness, our awareness that we answer to a divine Creator. It can often be suppressed but never fully ignored. Even the atheist has it. If in this awareness a person fails to acknowledge the Creator, they will be left with an emptiness that cannot be filled with anything else. The spirit is the vehicle to communicate with God.

We are all aware of our body and its functions. Therefore, it is not part of our discussion, since this information can be found in the study of anatomy and physiology. Our trouble is differentiating between the soul and spirit. If the Word of God differentiates between soul and spirit, then we ought to as well. Over the years I have found that many Christians are unable to distinguish between these two.

It can safely be said that when the Enemy attacks, he will do so through the soul, whereas, when God speaks to us, He will do so through our spirit. If we have not learned to differentiate between the two, we will not be able to discern what comes from God, and what comes from the Enemy, or what originates from ourselves.

The Soul

The soul has three functions: the Intellect (mind), the Emotions, and the Will (volition).

The Intellect

This is where our thinking process takes place. Thoughts can only come from three possible sources. God can give me a thought. I can choose to think a thought, or the Enemy can impose a thought. There is no other source from where thoughts come. For example, I can give you an idea, but I cannot project a thought into your mind and make you believe that you are thinking it. God could give me a thought. However, if God were to impose a thought in my mind, I would believe it to be my own, since it happens in my mind and I would act upon it. But by doing this, God would be treating me like a robot. God has limited Himself by giving us a free will, not to impose thoughts. God communicates directly to our spirit.

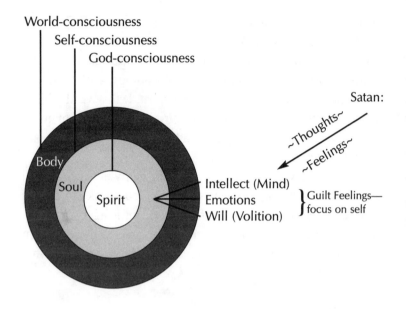

Figure 5.2 - The Soul

Our mind is an inappropriate tool for understanding God. For example, if we have an electric light bulb and there is power in the electrical outlet, we can connect two strings to the light bulb and to the outlet, but we will fail to get the bulb to light up. The strings cannot conduct electricity; we need wire. In the same way, our minds cannot directly understand God because He is so far beyond our mind's capability.

If this is true, then there are now only two possible sources from which thoughts originate. Either they originate from me, and I choose to think them, or the Enemy imposes thoughts. We must take into consideration the fact that the devil does not want us to have a free will, but wants us to operate like robots.

Which things also we speak, not in the words which man's wisdom teacheth, but which the Holy Ghost teacheth; comparing spiritual things with spiritual. But the natural man receiveth not the things of the Spirit of God: for they are foolishness unto him: neither can he know them, because they are spiritually discerned (1 Corinthians 2:13-14).

The mind is part of the natural man and therefore cannot receive the things of the Spirit of God. Spiritual things are spiritually discerned. We cannot use our minds to understand the things of God directly. The Holy Spirit, through our spirit, must reveal them to us.

We have a clear example of this notion in Scripture when Jesus told the disciples He was going to die on the cross. Peter said, "Don't let this happen, Lord!" And Jesus replied, *"Get thee behind me, Satan"* (Matthew 16:23.) Why didn't Jesus say, "Get thee behind me, Peter?" Peter said it and thought that it was his own thought, but Jesus recognized that it was the devil giving him those words, and so commanded the devil, instead of Peter. If the devil could speak through Peter, then he can speak through and to any one of us, as the following examples show.

A student named Kerri came to see me. She was short and a little chubby, but certainly not fat. Kerri shared with me that she had struggled with a poor self-image all her life. "…And then my weight adds to the problem." I said to her, "Kerri, that is a symptom, but not the real problem or the cause of your poor self-image."

Kerri then remembered that when she was three years old, her mother had her two-year-old sister on one knee and a new baby on her other. Being only three, Kerri wanted to be picked

Her mother said, "No, you are too heavy." That sin-
..ent had stayed with her all these years. Now, Kerri's
..adn't intended to imply that she was too fat, but that
she s..nply didn't have room for her. She could have communicated it in many different ways, but I believe that the devil had
the mother say those words to make her three year old believe
she was unlovable because she was too fat.

Similarly, Harvey, a man in his sixties, had felt all his life
that he was a dummy. Although he was a spirit-filled Christian,
he was unable to believe that God could use him. This feeling
was so strong that Harvey wouldn't even pray aloud in public.
When I probed for background, Harvey began to relate how he
had had the same teacher from grades two through seven, and
he never knew why the teacher didn't like him. This teacher was
very strict and harsh, and Harvey was afraid of him. The teacher
would ask the students to memorize a poem. Harvey would go
home and memorize it, but when he came to the classroom, his
mind would go blank. The teacher would spank him for being
lazy and disobedient and called him the "class dummy."

Now he was a successful farmer, yet could not believe
that he was intelligent or even useful. I told him that this was
a lie. 2 Timothy 1:7 reads, *"For God hath not given us a spirit
of fear, but of power, and of love, and of a **sound mind**"*
[emphasis mine]. Therefore, for Harvey to believe that God
hadn't given him a sound mind was to believe the lie the
Enemy fed him through his teacher. I guided Harvey to ask
forgiveness for having believed that lie and commanded the
Enemy to leave him and not to return.

When I commanded the Enemy to leave, nothing happened immediately. The next day at noon I met Harvey again
and asked him how he was. He said, "What a night!" I had
assumed that because we had exposed the Enemy, he was

stirred up and had really started attacking Harvey, until he told me what had happened. He couldn't sleep, and God began to show him incidents from his childhood.

God reminded him about when he was just a young boy. Harvey's father would have him drive wild, hard-to-handle horses, while his father would sit calmly in the back seat. God spoke to his spirit, "Just as your dad trusted you to handle those wild horses, I am trusting you to do things for Me." With that, an emotional dam of pent-up hurt feelings broke. He said, "I cried all night, and I cried all morning in the barn." From that time on, he no longer believed that he was a dummy. Harvey was so free that, afterwards, he went to different countries to share the gospel.

If a mentally-handicapped person is told he is stupid, it doesn't hurt him because he doesn't understand. However, when an intelligent person is told that he is stupid, it hurts deeply and these hurts can accumulate one on top of the other, year after year, until he is unable to see what is true.

With so many people, the Enemy uses thoughts of inferiority to make us believe in. When we believe his lies, we strive to compensate, withdraw, or make a host of other attempts to cope and coexist with our "problem." So many people suffer from this kind of bondage. Therefore, we need to learn to discern what is a lie and what is truth.

We need to identify the source of our thoughts. I teach two ways of identifying them. The first way to discern the origin of a thought is to determine whether the thought is a voluntary one. For example, if I want to think about my house, I can do so. If I want to think of clothes, I can do so. If politics is something that I want to think about, then I will. However, if I don't want to think of clothes again today, I don't need to. Thoughts that originate from me, I am in control of and can change at will.

et's say that somebody hurts me and I am aware of thoughts of revenge. However, as a Christian, I have determined not to think this way. If I choose to think of something else, and five minutes later, those revengeful thoughts are back again, then obviously they are being imposed upon me. I may think that those thoughts originated from me, just as Peter did when Jesus said, "Get thee behind me, Satan," but they don't. If I have accepted these as my own thoughts, I will feel guilty and will try harder and harder to forgive or stop thinking those revengeful thoughts. It is important that I know and understand that I am not dealing with flesh and blood, but rather with principalities and powers that are imposing these thoughts on my mind. They are not originating from myself, because if I choose when to start thinking the thoughts, I can also choose when to stop thinking them.

The second way of discerning the lies imposed by Satan is to recognize that when negative thoughts regarding myself come with the personal pronoun "You," such as, "You're lazy!," "You're stupid!," "You're wicked!," "You shouldn't have done that!," it's the Enemy speaking. It's a dead-give-away. It is not "me" speaking, but someone else, because if it were me speaking, then I would use the pronoun "I," not "You."

A mother brought her fourteen-year-old son, Kenny, to see me. He was constantly getting into fights at school. The principal suspended him because he was concerned in light of the recent Littleton, Colorado massacre, that something more serious might happen. The principal told the family to take the young man for counseling.

Kenny came and shared with me that for the past two years, he hadn't wanted to live. From all appearances, it looked as if this were the truth. I told him that he had believed a lie because God had created us with a desire to live. However, this young

66

man could not see that it was a lie. I said to him, "Kenny, what if you and I became aware that this whole house had become engulfed in flames, what would you do?" Without hesitation he said, " I would jump out the window!" I replied, "Now, if you don't want to live, why then would you jump out the window?" He pondered it for a number of seconds and all of sudden a big smile burst out all over his face. I could see that the lie was broken, and he said with excitement, "I want to live!"

Kenny had to see me on a regular basis, but instead of counseling him, he would share with me reports of praise and testimonies of what God was doing in his life. His mother said, "I can hardly believe the change in my son! Before, unless I really got mad, I couldn't get him to do anything. Now he offers to do things without being asked." One week when he came, he confessed he had a bad day and had a fight with his sister. After this had happened the thought came to his mind, "You should go to the bathroom and take some pills," but he caught the "You" and said, "Devil, if you want to take pills, go right ahead, but I'm not!" With that, the temptation was gone!

Similarly, several years ago, I did a seminar in Montana on this teaching. After I had finished speaking for the weekend, they had me booked for counseling. A middle-aged man named Walter came and told me that he had a tumour in the bone of his leg, but the doctor had refused to operate until he quit smoking because smoking would hinder the healing. Walter, therefore, quit smoking and had the operation, but now, there was such a strong urge to smoke, it almost drove him out of his mind. Walter had heard my teaching on how the Enemy works and about the seven steps to freedom, which I will share in the following chapter. We proceeded immediately to work through the seven steps. We had just started on step one, when our counseling session was interrupted, and we had to reschedule for the next day.

When Walter came back the next day, he had an interesting story to share. After he left my office, he had no urge at all to smoke, and the thought that came to him was, *See, 'you' don't have to go and finish the seven steps, 'you' are free already.* After the thought came several times, he caught the 'You' and said, "Devil, I'm going back to finish these steps to freedom." Then the urge to smoke came over him with unbelievable intensity.

Often when I ask people whether the negative thoughts come as "You" or "I," some immediately recognize that they come as "You," but others when they think about it believe that it's "I." However, when I challenge them to really pay attention to negative thoughts, all of sudden they realize that they do come as "You." The devil will sometimes use "I" thoughts as well, but these are not so easily discerned.

 The devil cannot read our thoughts because he is not all-powerful (omnipotent) or all-knowing (omniscient). However, he does know human behaviour, and he can see by our actions and by our speech whether or not we believe what he has told us. If he has just told you that you are "good-for-nothing" or that you are ugly, and he sees that you are stooped-over with your heart in the gutter, then he knows you have accepted his thoughts.

The Emotions

Not only does the devil impose thoughts directly into our intellect, but he often imposes feelings on our emotions as well. Some people are gripped by a spirit of fear and are almost incapacitated, and yet they don't even know what they are afraid of. This clearly shows that the spirit of fear is imposing that feeling. Most often, the Enemy imposes both thoughts and feelings.

Imposed feelings are very convincing because the feelings happen right inside the emotional part of our being. Coupled with the fact that the world tells us to trust our feelings, we are easily fooled. The devil can really take us for a ride when he convinces us that the feelings he has imposed, originated with us.

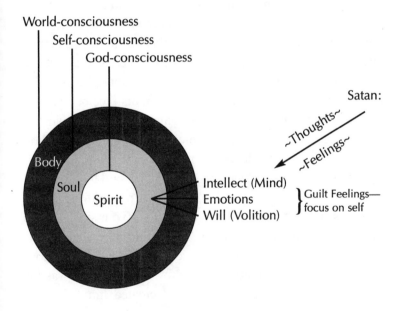

World-consciousness
Self-consciousness
God-consciousness

Body
Soul
Spirit

Satan:
~Thoughts~
~Feelings~

Intellect (Mind)
Emotions
Will (Volition)

} Guilt Feelings—
focus on self

Figure 5.3 - The Emotions

For example, if a hiker goes into the bush and sees a bear, he will experience fear. This is a healthy, God-given fear because it's best to get out of the way of a bear. On the other hand, when the hiker goes into the bush when it is getting dark and sees a dark object that he believes is a bear, it produces the same fear. If somebody comes and shines a light on that dark object and the hiker sees that it is only a tree stump, the fear no longer has power over him. This helps us understand John 8:32: *"And ye shall know the truth, and the truth shall make you free."* As long as that hiker believes that the tree stump is a bear, it might as well be. A lie believed as truth has the same power as if it were true.

A man in ministry came to see me. He told me that he had been filled with lust ever since he had been in grade one. To me this was an immediate indication that this feeling was demonic, because at six years of age, a boy does not have sexual lust.

He told me that whenever he saw a woman, he mentally undressed her. Afterwards, he fell flat on his face before God and repented, but he would do it again with the next woman he saw. He had fought this problem for thirty years, feeling guilty and ashamed. He asked me, "What if the people supporting me knew what was on my mind?" I said to him, "You are not confessing your sin, but you're confessing the demon's sin, and that does not set you free. Your sin is not the lust. Because you are *fighting* it, how could it be yours? Your sin is that you *believe* that this is your lust." That day, he confessed his sin of dishonouring God by believing this was his lust and for believing that God had created him this way. Needless to say, God forgave him.

When I met him the next day, he was all smiles. He said to me, "For the first time in my life, my mind is clear!" This remained true, even though there were many women around him. It was the Enemy who had given him the imagination and the feeling of lust, and as long as he believed it was his own, it controlled him.

70

The first sin in the Garden of Eden was not the eating of the fruit. The first sin was believing the devil's lies. The devil said, *"God knows the day you eat thereof, you shall be like God"* (Genesis 3:5). When Eve believed she could have something good for herself apart from God, she rejected what God had said and believed the devil's lie. That was her sin. This belief gave the devil power in her life, and she then looked at the fruit and desired it. She must have seen that fruit many times before because the tree was right in the middle of the Garden. It was after she believed the lie that she felt desire towards the fruit. Likewise, when we believe the devil's lies, no matter how logical they seem, it gives the Enemy power in our lives. **It is important to see that in order to believe the devil's lies, we have to reject God's truth.**

The Bible says that Eve was deceived, and Adam was not deceived. 1 Timothy 2:14 reads, *"And Adam was not deceived, but the woman being deceived was in the transgression."* If Adam knew that the devil was lying, why then did Adam take of the forbidden fruit? Eve made a decision to disobey God based on the lies fed to her. If Adam had chosen to stay true to God, he would have been separated from Eve.

The devil likely increased Adam's feeling of attraction to Eve to such an extent that Adam felt there was no way he could be separated from Eve. Based on his strong emotional attraction to Eve, he chose to disobey. Adam was influenced through his emotions, and Eve through her intellect.

Have you ever had to fight something you knew was wrong? You didn't want it, and yet it was so overpowering? If you can recognize that the thoughts or feelings are not coming from you, then you can get a handle on the problem.

An elder's wife named Kim came for counseling. She had been oppressed for all fourteen years of her marriage. A wall went up between her and her husband on their wedding day, and she could not bear to have him touch her. She explained that whenever he touched her anywhere, it felt like knives pricking her, and she would recoil. She tried to climb over that wall, but couldn't. He read her response as rejection. He didn't understand, and she didn't understand it either. It was a miracle their marriage was still together.

We discovered a man-hating demon who was violent. It would lunge at me through her and say, "I'm going to kill you!" She was a short woman, but because of the demon, she possessed super-human strength and would attack me.

It seemed that every time I shared truth with her, or if a lie was being exposed, the demon would take over, stalling for more time. For all those years, the demon had been hiding behind her personality, and she thought that she was weird because of what was happening inside her. She had tried hard to change, but to no avail.

After she had attacked me a number of times, I said to her, "Kim, are you aware when the demons are about to take over?" She said, "Yes." So, I said, "When you sense they are going to take over, give me your hands. It'll be easier on me and on you." The next time, just as I was sharing some truth, she gave me her hands and none too soon!

After the demon released her, Kim said to me, "It was so hard to give my hands to you. It was like an act of submission." "What do you mean?" I asked. She said, "The emotion of destruction is so strong and pleasurable, I long to give into it." She had no desire to torture or kill me. She appreciated me. Why, then, was she feeling pleasure?

As the demon planned to attack me through her, it was anticipating the pleasure of doing that to me, and she was aware of that pleasure. It was a demon's pleasure that she experienced, and that is why it was so hard for her to give me her hands. It is essential to remember that the pleasure did not originate from her. It was imposed on her by the demon. ✗

One time, when both her husband and I had to hold Kim down, the demon stopped struggling, although it had not left. The demon showed its contempt by making an ugly face towards her husband. Now, this did not affect me, for I knew that it was the demon in her doing this. At that moment, however, Dave felt anger rise up in him against his wife, and at the same time, the demon spoke audibly from her, "Hit her, hit her!" What a set up!

How did that demon in her know that Dave was feeling anger and repulsion towards his wife? Either that demon in her was projecting it onto him, or there were two demons working together. Can you see why families break up, thinking they are fighting each other, when in reality, it is a spiritual battle?

Her husband Dave finally saw what he had been up against all these years. He had been battling with flesh and blood and saw only rejection through it. He now saw that it was the demon rejecting him and that Kim had never rejected him. He was overwhelmed with love for his wife when he understood the turmoil that she had gone through for the past fourteen years.

Michael, a brilliant young man of thirty years, came to see me. He told me that ever since he had been in grade one, he had an attraction towards boys and never had any attraction towards girls. For many years, he thought he was just weird and so didn't talk about it. It wasn't until he was about twenty that he became involved in homosexuality.

One day, while he was walking in a strange city, it was almost as if a force took him and pushed him into an unknown building. When he got inside, he saw that it was a homosexual club. Ever since that day, Michael couldn't break with the homosexual involvement.

Michael, who was a sincere Christian, said to me, "I know that this is an abomination to God. I've made covenants before God and other men that I will not do it again, but it overpowers me." I said to Michael, "God has created you with a normal sexuality. He has created us with normal emotions and drives, but we are created to be in control of them, instead of them controlling us." I continued to explain to Michael how God has given us a hunger drive, but on a day-to-day basis, we are in control. We can decide to fast for a day or so, or we can take double desserts. An anorexic believes she is in control, but she is not. She can only say 'no!' to food. An overeater can only say 'yes' to food; an outside force controls both. The devil's tactic is to make us believe that this is our problem or our desire. In a similar way, God has given each person a sexual drive, and we are able to say 'yes' or 'no' to it. In Michael's case, there was a homosexual demon with such a strong, lustful drive that it was blanking-out the weaker, God-given heterosexual drive. To illustrate, if I have a scratch on my arm that is painful, but then I break my arm, I won't feel the scratch any longer because the greater pain of the broken arm overrides it. In the same way, a homosexual is not aware of his heterosexual drive because the homosexual drive that the Enemy imposes on him is stronger than the God-given heterosexual drive.

After I had shared this, Michael's eyes just lit up, and he said, "Then, I am not a homosexual!" I said, "That's right!" He then really got excited, "Then I am a heterosexual!" I laughed and said, "That's correct!" A couple of weeks later, he telephoned me back and said, "For the first time in my life, I have a desire to get married." This proved that his God-given heterosexual drive had been there all along, but he had

never been aware of it because the drive the de
was so much stronger. A year later, Michael sent
that said it had been the best year of his life. In 1
getting married in three months! God never gives us drives or
emotions that control us. If we can't control them, then it is a
clear indication that the Enemy has imposed it.

The Will

As the diagram shows (p.69), the third function of the
soul is the will, or volition. I'm not talking about willpower
here, but about making choices whether to believe a lie or the
truth. If we want to change something and can't change it
with willpower, then we are up against a different power,
namely, Enemy-power. We then have the choice of believing
that this is the Enemy or ourselves. If we choose to believe it
is ourselves and are not able to change our situation with
willpower, then we will feel defeated, discouraged, and in
bondage. But Romans 8:2 teaches us, *"For the law of the
spirit of life in Christ Jesus hath made me free from the law
of sin and death."* In understanding this verse, we see we are
not trying to fight to *get* victory. Rather, we are fighting from
the *position* of victory. When we fight to get victory, we've
already lost victory. We've lost it because we've failed to recognize that in the particular area we're struggling with, Christ
has already been victorious, and we have failed to see that He
lives in us. When we fight from the position of victory, we
then rely on the fact that the demon is already defeated, and
we can stand on that truth. If we say, "The devil made me do
it," we are incorrect because the devil can only have power if
we believe the lie he fed to us. *We* are still responsible.

The Bible consistently challenges us to choose to exercise
our will: *"Choose this day, whom you will serve"* (Joshua

24:15). The choice is ours, but if we believe the devil's lies and see the situation through his perspective, we are in bondage. However, if we choose to believe God's truth and choose to see it through His perspective, we are free. Romans 6:16 says,

Know ye not, that to whom ye yield yourselves servants to obey, his servants ye are to whom you obey; whether of sin unto death, or of obedience unto righteousness?

To yield ourselves is a decision, which is an exercise of the will.

When Christians are struggling or are going through trials, other well-meaning Christians will often advise them to "Keep looking up," thinking they are giving them good advice. But this is actually bad advice. Better advice would be to "Keep looking down." To illustrate, if we stand beside a thirty-story building and look up at the building, the building looks huge. From that perspective, an airliner thirty thousand feet up looks very small. In contrast, from up in that airliner, the plane looks large and that building is but a dot.

If we are struggling in a trial and are looking up from underneath that problem, our problem looks huge and God looks far away and small. Ephesians 2:4-6 tells us,

But God... even when we were dead in sins, hath quickened us together with Christ, (by grace ye are saved;) And hath raised us up together, and made us to sit together in heavenly places in Christ Jesus.

When we see things from this position, of sitting in heavenly places, we are seeing things from God's perspective. We will then see that He has a purpose He wants to accomplish in us through the trial. When we are viewing things from above from our position with Christ, it is God who looks big problem small.

We have the choice to see any circumstance through either the Enemy's perspective or through God's. We are not a victim; we are more than a conqueror! (Romans 8:37). The only reason we believe we are victims is because we believe the lies of the Enemy. The devil's tactics have never changed. He put man in bondage in the Garden of Eden by getting him to believe his lies, and he still uses the same method to defeat us. Many people say, "I don't like to think about the devil." Not thinking about him does not mean he is going to go away. If we don't stand against his lies with God's truth, we lose by default because he takes every opportunity to defeat us.

The story of God throwing the devil out of Heaven is in Isaiah 14. The devil hates God in the worst way. Since God is all-powerful, the devil can't fight God directly (although he is very powerful in his own right), and so instead, he torments God's children. In that way, he gets back at God because he knows it hurts God when His children reject His truth and instead believe the devil's lies. If we believe that by ignoring the devil the problem will go away, we are wrong. The devil does not ignore us, but takes advantage of the fact that we ignore him. The devil is not a passive Enemy. When he tells us a little lie, we may be tempted to think, "It's not a big deal—there is not much harm done by believing that little lie." However, as we go along, we get further and further from the truth. For example, if a person aims a rifle at a target and moves his sights even a fraction of a degree, he will still hit a target ten feet away. But shoot this shot at the distance of a mile and the bullet will be way off course. Likewise, we may not see the immediate consequences of a "little lie," but the end result is bondage.

The Spirit

Which things also we speak, not in the words which man's wisdom teacheth, but which the Holy Ghost teacheth; comparing spiritual things with spiritual. But the natural man receiveth not the things of the Spirit of God: for they are foolishness unto him: neither can he know them, because they are spiritually discerned (1 Corinthians 2:13-14).

God is a Spirit: and they that worship him must worship him in spirit and truth (John 4:24).

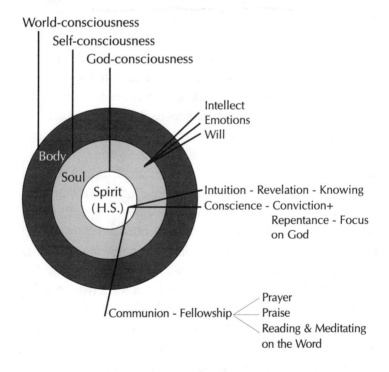

Figure 5.4 - The Spirit

When God desires to speak into our lives, He chooses to do so directly through our spirit: *"Spiritual things are spiritually discerned"* (1 Corinthians 2:14). I am so glad that God doesn't come through the same avenue as the devil, which is through our soul. It is not that our soul is useless, but it has to be governed through our spirit, and not vice versa.

Much like the soul, the spirit also has three functions: *intuition, conscience,* and *communion.*

The Intuition

By using the term intuition, I am not speaking of what we know to be a "woman's intuition," but rather, what is God's revelation to us.

I grew up in a Christian home and was taught the way of salvation since I was a child. I never questioned the fact that Jesus died for my sins or that He had paid the price with His own blood. But although I believed those facts, they were not real to me. It wasn't until I was in my early twenties that I actually chose to appropriate these truths. Then God made it real to me. His Spirit bore witness with my spirit that I was a child of God (Romans 8:16). Then I knew, that I knew, that I *knew*!

If somebody wants to wait until he can understand the way of salvation with his mind before he accepts it, it will never come. We must choose to accept a Biblical truth, and then God reveals it to our spirit. How can we tell the difference between whether we strongly believe the thing with our mind, or whether we received it through revelation?

Let's suppose that we have been taught a certain form of baptism since childhood, believe that it is the right way, and never question it. Then one day, someone comes along and says that our view is not what the Bible teaches. Immediately, we will be defensive and will try to show that person he is wrong and that *we* are right. However, when we have received something by revelation, we don't feel a need to defend it. If somebody says to us, "You can't know you are saved and are going to go to Heaven," we have no need to defend it because we *know* the truth in our "knower." Romans 8:16 confirms that, *"The Spirit itself beareth witness with out spirit, that we are children of God."*

Our part is to believe God's Word. God's part is to reveal it to our spirit and give us the faith. Hebrews 11:1 tells us, *"Now faith is the substance of things hoped for, the evidence of things not seen."* Faith is substance. It is not just believing something is real, but *knowing* it's real. When God reveals something to our spirits, and our minds immediately grasp it as well, it may seem to us that it came through the mind, but this is not the case. Sometimes we know that God is saying something to our spirit—we sense it—but our minds don't yet grasp it. It may take a week or a year before we hear or read something that allows our minds to grasp it as well. There can be a big gap between the time God first shows us something to our spirit and when we actually catch on to it with our minds. Our minds need to understand after the revelation, or we would otherwise be unable to share it with others. If we try to explain a spiritual truth, we have to be able to put that truth into words. We need our minds to do this. However, if we first try and understand with our mind before we receive it through our spirit, we will never, ever get it. This is a case of "putting the cart before the horse."

Our part is to read the Word of God and choose to believe it. Then God makes it real to us. Our choosing to believe the Word frees God to reveal it to us without imposing on our free will. Sometimes people will say, "I want to forgive somebody," or "I want to trust God," and they will even express their prayers in this way. Immediately, I stop them and say, "What good is that, just *wanting* to?" We must choose to forgive or choose to trust and allow God to work on our behalf, without violating our free will. If we wait until we *feel* like forgiving somebody, the Enemy will make sure the feeling will never come. However, after we *choose* to forgive, God can work out the rest in our lives. We are so used to going by feelings and accepting that all the feelings we are aware of are originating from us, that it hinders us from believing the truth of God that would set us free.

The Conscience

Most people believe that guilt feelings come through the conscience, but this is incorrect. Romans 8:1 clearly states,

> *There is therefore now no condemnation* [guilt] *to them which are in Christ Jesus, who walk not after the flesh,* [the soul] *but after the Spirit.*

This verse shows us that God does not use guilt or condemnation. Romans 2:4 tells us what God does use:

> *Or despisest thou the riches of goodness and forbearance and longsuffering; not knowing that the* **goodness of God** *leadeth thee to repentance?* [emphasis mine].

The devil is the one who comes with guilt and condemnation, and that comes through the soul via our intellect and emotions. (See the diagram on the soul, p.62.) This happens when he succeeds in having us focus on self. He imposes thoughts on us that, we shouldn't have done a certain thing, or that we should have done another thing, or that God can't forgive a sin that is so horrible, etc. If we believe those s, then the guilt stays with us. We may confess them, when the feelings of guilt from the Enemy remain, we don't feel forgiven and, therefore, believe that God has not really forgiven us. So, again, we go by the feelings and not by the fact given to us in 1 John 1:9 which says, *"If we confess our sins, he [God] is faithful and just to forgive us our sins, and to cleanse us from all unrighteousness."* We need to *choose* to believe the Word of God rather than the feelings that we are aware of. We need to learn to use the expression, "These feelings that I am aware of," rather than, "This is the way I feel." We should not take ownership of imposed feelings. If we acknowledge them as ours, we are giving the Enemy power in our lives.

> *For as the heaven is high above the earth, so great is his mercy toward them that fear him. As far as the east is from the west, so far hath he removed our transgressions from us* (Psalm 103:11-12).

So often, instead of trusting God's forgiveness when we confess our sin, we look at our feelings as evidence as to whether or not we are forgiven.

As I said before, I had been taught the way of salvation from childhood, so I knew that I had to confess I was a sinner and accept Christ's atoning work on my behalf. I didn't do it until my early twenties. When I actually did do it, I waited for the feeling of which others had testified—a euphoric "cloud nine" feeling. People would say that the grass looked greener and the sky looked bluer when they became saved. I did not have a "cloud nine" feeling, and the grass did not look any greener, nor the sky any bluer. I then concluded my transaction with God must not have worked. I had done what I had always known I should do, but it didn't work and, as a result, fear gripped me. *What if I had to go to Hell now because I didn't feel forgiven?* Every night I confessed my sins all over again, asking God to forgive me, but still no euphoric feelings came. I had no assurance of salvation. About two months later, I read a book which described the way I was feeling. The author wrote about noticing a difference in our desires after we are saved. The things we desired before, we now no longer desire. Moreover, the things we never had a desire for, we now do. [1]

The revelation hit me. I saw that I was trying to listen to every Christian broadcast that I could. I never had that desire before. Other things I used to desire had no claim on me anymore. Finally, I realized that God had saved me the first time I asked. However, I was waiting for the *feelings* as evidence, instead of *believing* the Word of God. Since the devil hinders us from feeling forgiven, we continue to carry the guilt of our sins and believe that God has not forgiven us.

So, if God does not use guilt feelings or condemnation, how does He deal with us? Looking back at the diagram of the spirit (p.78), we see that God comes with conviction. With the conviction, He gives us repentance, and this happens when we focus on God and not on self. When Isaiah saw the Lord, he said,

> *...Woe is me! for I am undone; because I am a man of unclean lips and I dwell midst a people of unclean lips: for mine eyes have seen the King, the Lord of Hosts* (Isaiah 6:5).

When we focus on God, we come into the light, and light exposes the darkness. We might believe we are pretty good people, but when we encounter God and His Word, the light will expose the areas of darkness in our heart: *"The heart is deceitful above all things, and desperately wicked: who can know it?"* (Jeremiah 17:9). It is both the Word of God and the Spirit of God that will expose our selfishness and sinfulness. We need to ask God to expose our heart instead of trying to search it ourselves. If we do the latter, the Enemy will accuse us of all sorts of things and will condemn us. We can sort and arrange piles of garbage any way we like; we can give them different titles, but it is *still* garbage. That is why the Psalmist emphasizes *God* searching, rather than "I" searching myself:

> ***Search me**, O God, and know my heart: **try me**, and know my thoughts: And see if there be any wicked way in me, and lead me in the way everlasting* [emphasis mine] (Psalm 119:23-24).

There is a simple way to differentiate between guilt feelings which come from the Enemy and conviction which comes from God. Guilt feelings are depressing, discouraging, and we feel down. Conviction, on the other hand lifts us up to a higher ground and is encouraging. As we see our sinfulness, we also see the forgiveness, and this brings true joy.

Communion

Communion means fellowship. Fellowship can be seen as two fellows being in one ship, a situation which enables them to get to know each other well. The way we can fellowship with God is through prayer—not just asking God for things, but waiting for Him to speak to us as well. We also fellowship with Him through praise, through reading and meditating on His Word, and through seeing God's hand in trials. Job, after he went through his trials said, "Until now I heard about You, but now, I am seeing You!" (Job 42:5).

Through communion, we get to know God and who He is, how much He loves us, how much He is concerned about us, and since He is Almighty, how much more He will take care of us, even more than He cares for the birds and the lilies:

> *And we know that all things work together for good to them that love God, to them that are called according to his purpose* (Romans 8:28).

If we really focus on God and who He is—the One who said, "Let there be light," and there was light—and if we know He lives in us, it is impossible to worry at the same time. He can surely handle any problem we may ever have to face. Therefore, if we worry, it shows that we have taken our eyes off God and put them on ourselves. We may not understand all that is happening, but we can always choose to trust.

If we are operating in the soul, where the Enemy imposes lies, it will be a downward spiral. We will become discouraged, distressed, and despondent.

But if we are functioning in the spirit, we will spiral upwards with God. As we have greater communion with Him, we will get more revelation in our intuition from Him. As we have more revelation from God, we will see more of our own sinfulness because we are coming into the light. We will be convicted in our conscience because of our sinfulness. Because we don't want anything between God and ourselves, we will repent, and He will forgive and cleanse us. This makes our fellowship closer than ever. It is truly a spiral upwards.

CHAPTER SIX

Seven Steps to Freedom

WHEN WE HAVE BELIEVED the devil's lies, we have sinned against God and have given the devil a legal right to build a stronghold in our lives. We need to break down that stronghold through the power of God. Over the past twenty-seven years of counseling, I have developed "Seven Steps to Freedom." These are steps that can show us how to take back the ground we have conceded to Satan. It is not enough to know about our sin, we also need to deal with it. These steps work in any area where the Enemy has a hold on our lives.

1. Identify the lie
2. Confess believing the lie as sin
3. Ask forgiveness for believing the lie
4. Thank God for the forgiveness
5. Take authority over the Enemy
6. Confess the truth in that area
7. Ask God to fill the released area with His Holy Spirit

1. Identify the Lie

The lie will come through thoughts and feelings. We will often need outside help, at this point, to help us identify the lie we have bought into. If we knew that something was a lie, we wouldn't believe it. Some of the previous examples I have shared show that this is true. A lie is exposed the moment it is brought into the light.

We will recall the story about Harvey, the man whose teacher said he was the "classroom dummy." He accepted this label as truth, and it affected and hindered him until he was in his sixties. He wasn't free until the lie was exposed in that area and he saw the truth.

The devil comes to steal, kill, and destroy, and he stole fifty years or more and destroyed many opportunities that Harvey could have been involved in, if he had not been governed by that lie. It took an outsider to help him see what the lie was and what the truth was.

2. Confess Believing the Lie as Sin

Believing a lie is a sin against God. We either directly or indirectly deny God's truth. If we believe we are stupid, then we are implying that God did not mean for us to have *"a sound mind"* (2 Timothy 1:7), or we are implying we are not *"fearfully and wonderfully made"* (Psalm 139:14). If we don't confess believing the lie as sin, then the devil keeps a foothold, and sin separates us from God.

3. Ask Forgiveness for Believing the Lie

If we confess our sins, he is faithful and just to forgive us our sins, and to cleanse us from all unrighteousness (1 John 1:9).

Today, the gospel is often presented without emphasizing the need for repentance, and seeks only to add Christ to our life so we can be happier now. However, if our sin is not removed, it separates us from God and gives the Enemy control, and he will continue to defeat us in that area we continue to sin in. At the root of the problem, there is a lie that has been believed. This is the sin. Often, we look at the result as being the sin. Rather, sin is the fruit of believing the lie. Thus, believing the lie must be confessed, and asking for forgiveness is mandatory.

4. Thank God for the Forgiveness

We need closure. We've brought our request for forgiveness to God and, now, we thank Him that He has taken over. This blesses God because it signifies that we are taking Him at His Word. He then gives us the "peace that passes understanding:"

> *Be careful for nothing; but in everything by prayer and supplication, with **thanksgiving** let your requests be made known unto God. And the peace of God, which passeth all understanding, shall keep your hearts and minds through Christ Jesus* [emphasis mine] (Philippians 4:6-7).

As long as we doubt, we won't thank God for taking care of the problem. If our feelings tell us we are still guilty, we will believe those feelings, and we won't want to thank God. By thanking Him, we are accepting that the sin is gone.

These first four steps take back the ground the devil had in our lives, due to our beliefs in his lies.

Sometimes people come to me, and they know they have demonic problems. They ask me if I would cast out these demons. I say, "No, I first want to know what you believe." If they believe lies of the devil, then they are giving him a legal right to keep themselves in bondage. If I am saying, "Devil, go!" when they are in fact saying, "Devil, stay!" we are not going to accomplish much—at least nothing permanent. However, if, through these first four steps, they take back the ground they had given the devil, we then, in the Name of Jesus, have the authority to command him to go.

5. Take Authority

In Luke 10:19, Jesus says,

Behold, I give unto you power to tread upon serpents and scorpions [demons], and over all the power of the enemy and nothing shall by any means hurt you.

We have to choose to believe that this authority is now ours, just as Jesus said. Demons like to intimidate; they pretend they still have power in order to keep us from walking in that authority. They are like a cat when it is confronted by a dog—it makes its hair stand on end to make itself appear bigger than it really is. In reality, the cat is no bigger. Similarly, the demons are defeated. All we need to do is to stand on that fact, and they have to yield. Jesus said, "*In my name, shall they cast out devils*" (Mark 16:17).

At the name of Jesus every knee should bow… and… every tongue should confess that Jesus Christ is Lord… (Philippians 2:10,11).

When I spoke in the name of Jesus, one demon said, "Leave Him [Jesus] out of it, and I am going to beat you." I said, "I agree, but I am not leaving Jesus out of this!"

Once we have removed any obvious roadblocks, we can proceed to take the authority, saying,

"In the name of Jesus, I break the power that this lie gave the Enemy in my life, and I command him to leave."

6. Confess the Truth in That Area

Ye shall know the truth, and the truth shall make you free (John 8:32).

It is hard to know what is a lie if we don't know what the truth is in that area. Usually, we can find Scriptures that speak about the issue. For example, if the devil has told us we are no good, we can choose to confess the truth and agree with God in what He says:

I will praise thee; for I am fearfully and wonderfully made (Psalm 139:14).

Therefore if any man be in Christ, he is a new creature: old things are passed away; behold all things are become new.... that we might be made the righteousness of God in him (2 Corinthians 5:17,21b).

We must actively choose to agree with those Scriptures and stand on those Scriptures. This is why it is essential to know the Word of God and to agree with it.

7. Ask God to Fill the Released Area with the Holy Spirit

When the unclean spirit is gone out of a man, he walketh through dry places, seeking rest; and finding none, he saith, I will return unto my house whence I came out. And when he cometh, he findeth it swept and garnished. Then goeth he and taketh to him seven

*other spirits more wicked than himself; and they enter
in, and dwell there: and the last state of that man is
worse than the first* (Luke 11:24-26).

We don't want that area left with an empty void, so we must ask God to fill the released area with the Holy Spirit.

When we have gone through the seven steps, we can really believe that the demon now has no ground in our lives. If we should get tripped up and unwittingly accept a lie again, then we simply go through the seven steps again. However, if we recognize the devil when he comes again with the same lie, and we reject it and stand on the truth, then we don't need to repeat the seven steps. Being tempted with a lie is not sin. It is the believing of the lie that is sin. Jesus was tempted by the same devil that Eve was tempted by, except Jesus didn't sin. He recognized that it was the devil that was speaking, and he simply answered, *"It is written...."*

CHAPTER SEVEN

Choosing God's Perspective

Neither yield ye your members as instruments of unrighteousness unto sin: but yield yourselves unto God, as those that are alive from the dead, and your members as instruments of righteousness unto God.... Know ye not, that to whom ye yield yourselves servants to obey, his servants ye are to whom ye obey; whether of sin unto death, or of obedience unto righteousness? (Romans 6:13,16).

ONE DAY WHEN I WAS meditating on Romans 6:13 and 16, I wondered what kind of "members" Paul was talking about. If we yield our members to the Enemy, we become his servants, and if we yield them to God, then we are His servants. What are these "members" we are reading about?

What was impressed on me was that the members are our mind and emotions. If we listen and believe the thoughts in our mind and take ownership of the feelings in our emotions that the Enemy gives us, then we become controlled servants of the

Enemy. We must recognize these as lies from the Enemy, yield ourselves to think godly thoughts, and present ourselves as a living sacrifice, holy and acceptable to God (Romans 12:1).

> *Be not conformed to this world: but be ye transformed by the renewing of the mind, that ye may prove what is that good and acceptable, and perfect will of God* (Romans 12:2).

How is the mind renewed?

> *Finally brethren, whatsoever things are true, whatsoever things are honest, whatsoever things are just, whatsoever things are pure, whatsoever things are lovely, whatsoever things are of good report; if there be any virtue, and if there be any praise, think on these things* (Philippians 4:8).

The decision is up to us—we can choose to allow the Enemy's thoughts and feelings to control us, or we can choose to think on the things of God.

The devil wants us to have a passive mind. This is why eastern religions and hypnotism are so dangerous. The Enemy can program us as he pleases if we have passive minds. God wants us to have active minds so we can *choose* to think what Jesus thinks, to agree on what He says, and thereby become victorious.

We can yield our thoughts and feelings as members either to sin or to God. God revealed to me an example of this. I mentioned earlier that you do not have to work on being angry. When I get up in the morning I don't say, "Today, I have to remember to get angry." If an irritation arises, the anger will surge through me just like propane released from a pressure tank. You do not have to pump propane out because

93

it is under pressure; all you have to do is open the valve, and the propane will gush out.

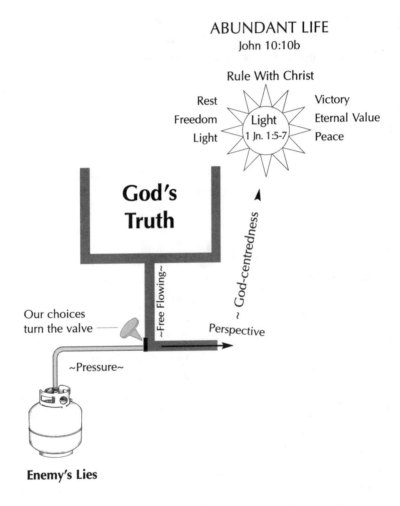

Figure 7.1 - Abundant Living

Two Tanks

Let's use a diagram by which to understand this concept better. Let's say we have a small pressure tank representing the Enemy's forces and a large gravity-flow tank representing God's truth. There is a valve with a lever in the middle of the two tanks, regulating the source of the flow.

These two tanks both connect into the same pipe at the valve. If you turn the valve fully to the left, the Enemy's tank is opened, and God's tank is closed. If you turn the valve fully to the right, then God's tank is opened, and the Enemy's tank is closed. If the valve is fully open to God and closed to the Enemy, the result is abundant living.

God never forces His way but allows it to "flow" through a receptive channel. In direct contrast, the Enemy uses pressure, much like a propane tank, to try to force us into a way of thinking and living.

We need to learn to keep our "valve" open to God in order to experience the blessings of walking in the Spirit. This is the intention of God, and it is in the person of Jesus where we have an example of this life.

But the fruit of the Spirit is love, joy, peace, longsuffering, gentleness, goodness, faith, meekness, temperance: against such there is no law (Galatians 5:22).

It is essential that we understand God's intention for man. When He created man, He planned that man would be God-centred and dependent on Him. If man had chosen to be totally God-centred and kept on choosing dependence on God, as Christ later did, man would have walked in all the fullness of God. Man would have had freedom, rest, peace, fruitfulness, etc. Man would have walked in the light as He is in the light.

This then is the message which we have heard of him, and declare unto you, that God is light and in him is no darkness at all. If we say that we have fellowship with him, and walk in darkness, we lie, and do not the truth: But if we walk in the light, as he is in the light, we have fellowship one with another, and the blood of Jesus Christ his Son cleanseth us from all sin (1 John 1:5-7).

We can see from this passage that if we are God-centred and walk in the light, we will have fellowship with God and with our fellow man. Jesus chose total God-centredness; He said only the things He heard His Father say, and did only the things He heard His Father tell Him to do. He chased the money-changers out of the Temple because they were making His Father's house *"a den of thieves"* (Matthew 21:13). Jesus was concerned for His Father, not for Himself. Therefore, He experienced the fullness and power of God all of His life. Jesus is the only person who has lived this life with the valve fully open to God, never accepting any of the lies of the devil, His life totally God-centred. Even when the devil tried to trip Him up, He maintained this abundant life perfectly. He just silenced the devil by saying, *"It is written..."*, leaving us an example of what we are to do when confronted with the Enemy.

However, this is not what Adam and Eve chose. Instead of shutting the devil up, they contemplated his enticing suggestions for self-centredness and thus introduced spiritual poverty into their lives, as well as spiritual death:

Because that, when they knew God, they glorified him not as God, neither were thankful; but became vain in their imaginations, and their foolish hearts became darkened (Romans 1:21).

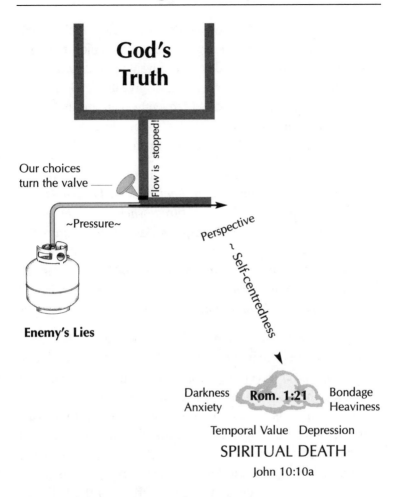

Figure 7.2 - Spiritual Death

Believing the devil's lies and agreeing with him released the devil's power in the lives of Adam and Eve, and this produced darkness in their hearts. Thus, the Enemy had the open door to impose anxiety, fear, guilt, bondage, defeat, and oppression.

Adam and Eve hid from God and felt ashamed of their naked-ness. By default, Adam and Eve gave the dominion they had over God's creation to the devil. God wants to be Lord of our lives, but by believing the devil's lies, we give the devil rulership and power over our lives and, subsequently, reap spiritual death.

This spiritual poverty could also be described as the works of the flesh and how they are manifested:

> *Now the works of the flesh are manifest, which are these; adultery, fornication, uncleanness, lascivious-ness, idolatry, witchcraft, hatred, variance, emula-tions, wrath, strife, seditions, heresies, envyings, mur-ders, drunkenness, revellings, and such like: of the which I tell you before, as I have also told you in time past, that they which do such things, shall not inherit the kingdom of God* (Galatians 5:19-21).

This verse is true of non-Christians. As they are born into Adam, they are born into deception. If they continue to live in deception, never accepting God's truth which can set them free, they shall not inherit the Kingdom of God.

All Christians have chosen to open the valve to at least some of God's truth, agreeing with God that they were sinners in need of a Saviour and accepting God's salvation. Now, the Holy Spirit, who wants to lead us into all truth, dwells in the believer's spirit, but doesn't force the truth on the believer. The devil, at the same time, tries to hinder us from living in the truth and power of God, by tempting us with the same temptations he gave Eve. This conflict and mixture is what all Christians experience to a greater or lesser degree.

If we have conditioned ourselves to believe the devil's thoughts and feelings when a situation arises, a choice will have to be made in order to agree with God's thoughts.

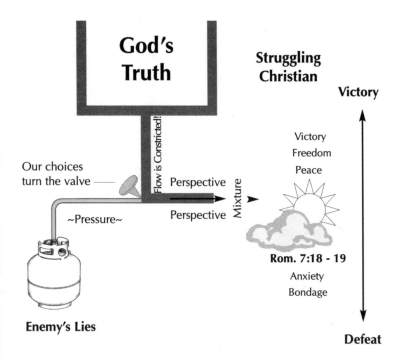

Figure 7.3 - The Struggling Christian

You may already recognize that the thoughts and the feelings you have accepted as truth in your life are lies, but unless you stop allowing them to flow through you unchecked, they will remain part of your automatic response. You have to say to yourself, "I recognize this is a lie, and I am not going to be controlled by it." Then, in essence, you have turned the valve and have chosen God's truth.

I grew up in a German-speaking community. I learned English in school, but did not get much practice speaking it in class because my overwhelmed teacher was barely able to keep the class under control, let alone help us practice our English. However, when I was in my twenties, I went to a Bible school where it was compulsory to speak English. I knew English and had read many English books, but I still *thought* in German.

Every time someone asked a question in English, the answer would automatically come to me in German. I would have to stop myself from answering in German and quickly translate it into English, often causing awkward sounding sentences. Nevertheless, over the course of time, I began to think in English and, therefore, I began to speak more fluently. In the same way, when we are used to allowing the thoughts and feelings of the Enemy to flow through us and have accepted them as our own, they do not automatically go away.

A lady who came to see me for counseling had extremely low self-worth. When I affirmed her in a certain area, she retorted angrily, "You don't know me. I am no good." She could only receive blame, and no credit. I asked her to write down five positive things about herself and hand them to me the next day. The following day she admitted that she could not do the assignment because she was unable to think of any positive qualities.

I related to her my experience of thinking in German. I said to her that she was thinking and speaking the devil's language. She had received the devil's degrading accusations and believed they were true for so long that now she was repeating the same accusations herself. I told her to stop speaking the degrading accusations when they came to her mind and then choose to speak the truths God says about her, such as: *"I am fearfully and wonderfully made"* (Psalm. 139:14), or *"I am a new creature in Christ Jesus, old things are passed away, behold all things are become new"* (2 Corinthians 5:17).

Eventually, she would begin to think in God's language and see herself from God's perspective.

To experience the life available to the believer, it is essential to be aware of which way the valve is turned. This "turning of the valve" is an exercise of discipline in choosing—a choice not to be controlled by the Enemy, and a choice to allow God's truth, and therefore God's power, to flow through us, allowing His life to be our life.

When we are aware of having failed, we should bring each situation to the cross and say, "Jesus, I recognize that what I believed in the past is a lie, and it is sin against you. I ask You to forgive me and cleanse me from all unrighteousness. I choose to think Your thoughts, to agree with You and what You say about this area." This turning of the valve to the other side is choosing the truth over the lie, and it has to be done through *discipline*. It will mean we will have to make a conscious decision to do this every time, until our response becomes automatic.

When I shared this in a group, a woman recalled the following experience: "There was a kid on our block who was so obnoxious that nobody could stand him. I was asked to babysit him for a whole week. After three days, the boy was driving me up the wall. I turned the valve by giving that situation over to God and, immediately, I felt such a love go through me for that boy, it was supernatural! I did not work on it, but it flowed through me, and to this day I am the only one who can relate to him on a deep level."

God wants His life to flow through us, but we must turn that valve and give up trying to use our willpower to live the Christian life. God never asked us to live the Christian life because He knows we cannot succeed. It is only as He lives His life *through* us that we can live the Christian life.

People are more overwhelmed with feelings than with thoughts. Christians can discern thoughts more clearly than they can discern their feelings. When a feeling hits you, it is automatic to believe that it is your own. The devil's power is in his ability to stay hidden. He wants you to remain in darkness, and as long as he can get you to believe that it is *you* feeling that way, when it really is *imposed* on you, then he will remain powerful.

This was illustrated in Grace, the first person I counseled. She had gone for secular counseling repeatedly, and the counselors believed that there was something seriously wrong with her. The demons remained hidden, but when I recognized that they were the cause of the problem, they knew they were exposed. Since there was no reason for them to remain hidden, they began to manifest quite openly.

Speak the truth. As you say it over and over again, it will become more and more real to you. At first it may seem a chore, just like it was a chore for me to speak English, but it will become easier.

A Christian lady came to see me. She felt unable to look at people directly because she said her eyes flicked back and forth. For nine years she refused to look people in the face because she was embarrassed. The truth was that her eyes never did flick back and forth. She had the sensation that this was happening, but in reality, it wasn't. I told her the truth, and she believed the truth and rejected the lie. After, she could look me straight in the eye, having no problem doing so. She was released from the lie.

Her second problem was with God. She said, "When I'm praising and worshipping Him I can sense such a love from God, and I know He is near, but why doesn't He protect me from all of this 'crap' that I'm going through? I can't bring the two together. How can a loving God leave me at the mercy of the Enemy?"

One morning, she came to my office and said, "God spoke to me this morning, but I don't understand it. He said that He would protect me through truth." To explain, I shared with her the following illustration:

If there is a bully at my daughter's school who teases her about her nose being too long, and she comes home crying day after day, I could intervene for her. I might go over there, grab him, and say, "If you do that one more time, I am going to bash your nose in." However, this would not help her in the long run because someone else might say something hurtful, and she would be in the same predicament.

Instead, I explain to my daughter that it doesn't matter what the bully says; he is the one with the problem. He has a need to put people down because of something hurtful in his own life. After she accepts the truth that she is special and that God created her "fearfully and wonderfully," the bully's teasing will not affect her. When he no longer gets a reaction from her, he will quit teasing.

The devil wants a reaction from the imposed thoughts and feelings he gives us. He wants to see rejection, self-pity, fear, etc. As long as we keep reacting, he will not stop because he is getting what he wants. We need to recognize the lie, refuse to react to it, ignore the devil, and then go one step further—confess the truth and rest in it.

Choosing Perspective

Perception is subjective, and perspective is objective. The Enemy tries to influence our perception in order for us to choose his perspective.

Adam and Eve chose to accept the devil's perspective

for their life, whereas Jesus chose the Father's perspective.

An anorexic has the devil-imposed *perception* of fat, and when accepted, it governs her *perspective* of herself as a person, thus destroying her self-image. It then produces a motivation to lose weight in order to be attractive and worthwhile.

Such imposed perceptions invade all areas of our lives, and when we accept them, believe them, and have chosen the devil's perspective in that area, they become the basis for our motivation and actions.

If we choose to see things through God's perspective, rather than through the devil's designed, imposed perception, then our motivation and action will come from the power of believing God's truth.

If we take a telescope and focus on an object many miles away, the telescope will magnify that object so it looks very near and large. However, turn that telescope around, looking through the wrong end, and focus on a nearby object—the telescope will cause that object to appear small and far away. Or, if we take a quarter and hold it directly in front of our eye, everything else will be blocked out, and the quarter will appear extremely large. From that perspective we might be tempted to believe the quarter is larger than even the sun, but our knowledge in the established facts of science would tell us that the sun is far larger than the quarter, despite the way it may appear to us at that moment. In a similar way, the devil can make a small problem look so large, that it totally distorts the reality of the situation.

The key to having God's perspective is in *knowing, believing*, and *agreeing* with the truth. What does God say about this particular area? When we know the truth, we are then able to make the decision to believe—but not only believe, but the decision or choice to agree. When we agree with the truth, our perspective is then in line with God's perspective.

In an earlier chapter, we referred to "looking down," as the correct viewpoint, implying that when we are agreeing with God's perspective, we are seeing things from His view point—the perfect overview. The lies of the Enemy then do not have any power.

In contrast, if we believe the imposed perception from the Enemy, we have then chosen to believe and agree with a lie. Thus, we give the devil the power to make that lie real in our life, thereby changing our perspective.

For our light affliction, which is but for a moment, worketh for us a far more exceeding and eternal weight of glory; While we look not at the things which are seen, but at the things which are not seen: for the things which are seen are temporal; but the things which are not seen are eternal (2 Corinthians 4:17-18).

Paul is speaking about two distinct perspectives—a *temporal* perspective and the glorious *eternal* perspective. When our perspective rests solely on the temporal, fleshly level, we will reap the works of the flesh. In contrast, if our perspective rests in the eternal—the things we cannot see but know, believe, and agree with—then we reap the fruit of the Spirit:

But the fruit of the Spirit is love, joy, peace, longsuffering, gentleness, goodness, faith, meekness, temperance: against such there is no law (Galatians 5:22).

It is very easy to agree with the Enemy because he not only appeals to our sense of the temporal, but he energizes the flesh and makes the lie so believable and often desirable.

To agree with God and His truth often requires a choice in opposition to our feelings and the appearance of things. But when we do, there is a release of God's power that enables that truth to become real in our lives.

A vivid illustration of the importance of perspective is the incident of the twelve spies whom Moses sent into the Promised Land (Numbers 13,14). They all saw the productive land, the same walled cities, and the same giants, but only two—Joshua and Caleb—had an opposite perspective from the other ten spies. The ten looked at the giants and then compared themselves with them. Compared to the giants, they saw themselves as grasshoppers. They depended upon their natural senses to evaluate the situation and, therefore, believed the perception imposed by the Enemy. They left God out of the equation.

Joshua and Caleb, on the other hand, compared the giants' size and strength to God, instead of to themselves. What a different perspective that produced! When the ten looked at the giants, they saw only defeat and death ahead. But when the other two viewed the giants, they saw them as *"bread for us"* (Numbers 14:9); seeing fighting those giants as an opportunity for growth. The ten viewed things through the devil's perspective, exhibiting their fear, while the other two revealed they were seeing things through God's perspective, showing their faith.

The outcome of these opposite perspectives also produced opposite results. The ten died immediately of a plague, whereas the two entered the Promised Land. Forty-five years later, after the Israelites had conquered the Enemy and were dividing the land, Caleb requested Joshua to give him the land where the giants dwelt. Caleb seemingly wanted more growth.

Similarly, in any trial or circumstance that confronts us, we have the choice of believing and accepting the negative perception the devil imposes on us, or we can choose to agree with God's positive perspective because *"...we know that all things work together for good to them that love God..."* (Romans 8:28).

By putting all three diagrams together, we get a full picture of the battle of the Christian life. (See p.108.) Jesus says in John 10:10a, *"The thief cometh not, but for to steal, and to kill, and to destroy."* The devil tries to produce spiritual death in us, as he did in Adam and Eve. In contrast, Jesus says in John 10:10b, *"I am come that they might have life, and that they might have it more abundantly."* Jesus does not push this on us, but wants us to ask for this and receive it as a gift. The devil, on the other hand, tries to push it on us by imposing deceptive perceptions, and then governing our perspective and motivation.

When we experience defeat, anxiety, bondage, and other negative states, we tend to see *these* as the problem, rather than the results or the symptoms of believing the wrong things.

After Adam and Eve had believed the devil's lies, they became anxious and tried to solve their anxiety by hiding from God. This is what we tend to do as well. Instead of looking to the truth and what we really believe and know, we tend to accept the devil's justification for feeling or acting a certain way. Following, is my own personal experience, as an example.

It's All Greek to Me

The Academic Dean at Living Faith Bible College, where I taught, came to me after the school year was finished and offered me the opportunity to join the Greek class he was going to teach in June. Some of the men on staff were working towards getting a degree from Living Faith Bible College, and he was going to teach them Greek from 7:00 to 8:00 in the morning. He knew that I had never taken any Greek for my degrees, so he said I could join the class because it was

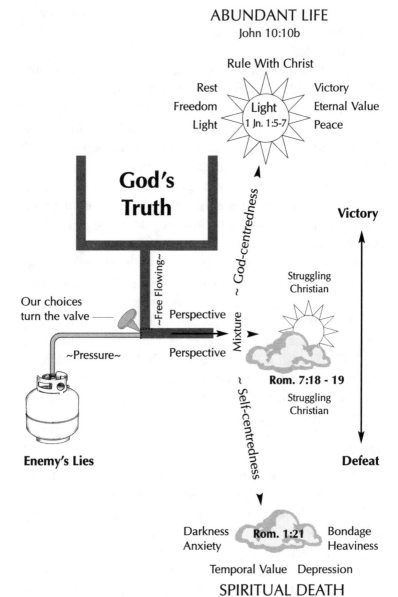

ABUNDANT LIFE
John 10:10b

Rule With Christ

Rest | Light | Victory
Freedom | 1 Jn. 1:5-7 | Eternal Value
Light | | Peace

God's Truth

Victory

~God-centredness~

~Free Flowing~

Perspective

Struggling Christian

Our choices turn the valve

Mixture

~Pressure~

Perspective

Rom. 7:18 - 19

Struggling Christian

~Self-centredness~

Enemy's Lies

Defeat

Darkness | **Rom. 1:21** | Bondage
Anxiety | | Heaviness

Temporal Value | Depression

SPIRITUAL DEATH
John 10:10a

Figure 7.4 - The Big Picture

no more work for him, and he was teaching the course anyhow. I was immediately concerned that, at my age, I might be unable to memorize a new language and keep up with the younger guys, but I decided it would be worthwhile to try. He told me they intended to begin the course in June.

When June arrived and I didn't hear anything, I kept on counseling. However, on June 6, I came to school in the morning at 8:00 a.m., as usual, and my son-in-law, Bob, who was also taking the course, met me and said, "Dad, why weren't you in class this morning?" I said, "Nobody told me we were starting today." He replied, "We were all wondering why you weren't in class."

A feeling of discouragement hit me and I had the thought, *Not only might my age be against me, but the others now have a head-start and the foundation of the language, and I haven't got it.*

I was in class the next morning at 7:00 a.m., only to find that the others had already learned the alphabet and had memorized the names and sounds of the letters the night before. Now, the Dean was putting Greek words on the blackboard, and the others were able to sound them out. I was unable to do anything because I had no idea what most of those letters were. The saying was never more true that it was "all Greek to me." I found myself thinking, *So, now I am wasting another class. They are benefitting from this, but I am not because I can't do it.*

A feeling of resentment hit me: *This is not fair! Because they didn't tell me when the class started, I am at a disadvantage! It's their fault!*

Before I could recover from the resentful feelings, thoughts of revenge hit me: *I am going to quit the course. I'll get up and walk out the door, but before I close the door and*

109

tell them I am quitting the course, I am going to make them feel bad for having done this to me. I knew this was an over-reaction; I also knew they had not done it on purpose. It was an oversight—after all, they were my friends and co-workers.

However, those feelings and thoughts did not quit. I chose not to quit the course while I was under attack from the Enemy because I did recognize that it had to have come from him. If after the attack was over I still wanted to quit the course, I could do so. Nobody was forcing me to take that course; I did it purely for interest's sake.

None of the others knew how I struggled sitting beside them. I literally held on to my chair to keep from getting up. I felt justified that they deserved to pay for their negligence.

Finally, 8:00 came, and it had been a very long hour. At 8:00, we start with prayer in the office, and I focused my mind on that. Then there was somebody waiting for counseling, and I had to concentrate on that. After I finished the counseling session, I met the Dean outside my office, and he offered to teach me the alphabet that I had missed the day before. He taught it to me, I went home and memorized it, and the next morning, I was up to par with the rest of them. In the end, I even received an A in that course!

I believe that God allowed the Enemy to attack me this way for three reasons: First, I could experience first-hand how real and overpowering these thoughts and feelings can be. Second, I had the opportunity to defeat the Enemy, and third, I had a new example that I could share with others.

Paul in Romans 7:18-19 shares a similar struggle:

For I know that in me, (that is, in my flesh,) dwelleth no good thing: for to will is present with me; but how to perform that which is good I find not. For the

110

*good that I would I do not: but the evil which I
would not, that I do.*

I am sure that we can all relate to these two examples.
Notice how easily the Enemy can impose negative thoughts
and feelings and then legitimize his plan of action for us. The
devil gave me such a strong urge to get even with "those
guys," and even gave me the plan of how to do it and feel justified that they deserved it.

Three Steps of Forgiveness

Another Biblical truth that further demonstrates how we can
turn the valve is the practice and application of forgiveness.

When we try to take authority over the Enemy in a particular area but have unforgiveness and resentment there, our
"take over" probably will not be successful. As Christians, we
know we have to forgive, but after we have done so, we often
are still not free. *Why?*

I believe there are three steps to forgiveness. If we *only*
forgive, God, through a sovereign act, sometimes sets us
totally free, but often we still struggle in that area or with
that person. Sometimes when an alcoholic is saved, he is
miraculously set free, yet another alcoholic, equally saved,
is not instantly set free. Does God have favourites? I
believe that the one who is miraculously set free will have
God use other areas in his life to teach him how to become
an overcomer. However, in the one who was not immediately set free, God may use the alcoholism to teach him to
become an overcomer. God knows which method works
best for each person.

The following chart is what I use to teach people how to
be totally free in a particular area:

Steps of Forgiveness:

1. Name of the Offender	2. The Offence	3. The Emotional Impact—hurt
Forgive the person.	Release the person from the offence; don't hold him accountable for that offence anymore.	Need healing; Receive the emotional healing by faith based on the fact that Jesus bore our grief and sorrows. (See Luke 4:18; Isaiah 53:3-4.)

The First Step: *Forgive the Person*

I suggest to the person that they ask God to bring to remembrance anyone they need to forgive, and then write the name of that person in the first column. In the second column, write down the offence(s), the negative thing(s) the person did or did not do, and the sins of commission or omission. They are to include perceived offences as well, even though the offender never intended them as an offence. In the third column, I have the person acknowledge the hurt the offence caused. The person is often most aware of the emotion of anger. However, underneath the anger there usually is deep hurt.

Jesus often stressed the need to forgive, and at one point said, "If you don't forgive, I won't forgive you!" (Matthew 6:15). If we wait to forgive until we *feel* like forgiving, we probably never will because the Enemy will make sure that the feeling will not surface.

112

The Second Step: *Release the person from the offence, and do not hold him accountable for that offence anymore.*

This is harder than just forgiving. Jesus practised this step when He hung on the cross. The first words He uttered on the cross were, *"Father, forgive them; for they know not what they do"* (Luke 23:34). If we look at Jesus' situation in the natural, it seems obvious that "they" knew exactly what they were doing. They were killing God's Son. However, Jesus saw that they were deceived. They believed that Jesus was an imposter and that they were helping God by getting rid of the imposter. If Jesus had only forgiven us for our sins but had not released us from our offences, we would still not be free.

If we do not release a person, then we are bound as well. One drama illustrated this point very clearly. The actor portrayed another person standing alongside him, who had deeply offended him. With one hand, he was holding the offending person by the neck, while telling him how wrong and unjust the offence was. He told the other person he had no right to do that to him.

Now the actor wished to do something that required the use of both his hands. However, he could not perform the task because his one hand was still holding the offender by the neck. This vividly illustrates that if we do not release the person who has offended us, then we are binding ourselves to them and, thus, we ourselves are not free.

The Third Step: *Receive emotional healing by faith.*

Once, when I was working on a house, I smashed my thumb with a hammer. Swollen and bruised, my thumb felt very painful and sensitive. The next day, it was incredible how often I bumped it. I probably bumped it just as often the day before, but never noticed it. Now, because it was sensitive, every *little* bump hurt just as much as the big bumps. But, once it was healed, I did not notice the little bumps any more.

In a similar way, our past hurts are sensitive and are prone to being bumped. The Enemy knows that the pain is there and so will use people or circumstances to re-open the wound. For example, if I was hurt deeply through rejection, then anything that even resembles rejection in the slightest way, could easily be read as rejection, and I could feel hurt all over again.

We are in need of emotional healing. We know that Isaiah 53:5—*"by His stripes we are healed,"*—refers to physical healing, but how do we receive emotional healing? In Luke 4:18, Jesus quotes from the book of Isaiah regarding Himself,

> *The Spirit of the Lord is upon me, because he hath anointed me to preach the gospel to the poor; he hath sent me to **heal the brokenhearted,** to preach deliverance to the captives and recovering of sight to the blind, **to set at liberty them that are bruised** [emphasis mine].*

The phrases, *"heal the brokenhearted"* and *"to set at liberty them that are bruised"* indicate that Jesus came to heal emotional pain. This list describes the full ministry of Jesus. Emotional healing is one of the reasons for His coming, and His purpose has never changed.

But how are we healed if He came to heal us? Isaiah 53:3-4 gives the answer. In verse 3 it says that He was a *"man of sorrows, acquainted with grief."* This definitely refers to emotional pain. Then in verse 4, we read that Jesus *"bore our grief and sorrows."* What does that mean for us that He "bore our emotional pain"? The Scriptures say that

Christ bore our sins in His own body on the cross. We don't have to bear our sins anymore because Jesus paid for them. Likewise, if He bore our griefs and sorrows, then I personally don't have to bear them anymore. Jesus bore the sins of every person, but only those who accept this fact by faith are set free from their sins. In the same way, Jesus bore every person's griefs and sorrows, but only when this is accepted by faith are we set free from emotional pain. We then will not be sensitive in that area anymore and will be able to function productively.

Shortly after I learned these truths about the "Three Steps of Forgiveness," a lady came to see me. She had undergone an emergency caesarean section the previous year. The doctors didn't think she would live through it, and neither did she. She did, in fact, survive, but according to her, due to the negligence of the doctors and nurses, the baby died. She was so resentful and angry, she went to a lawyer to have him draw up a case against the hospital.

After she shared her story, I taught these three steps of forgiveness. I then asked her to forgive the doctors and nurses and she did. But when I told her to *release* the doctors and nurses and no longer hold them accountable for their negligence, she said, "I can't do that!" I asked, "Why not?" She said, "Then they would be free." I said, "Yes, but you would be as well." It took me about twenty minutes to persuade her to release them. Finally, through an act of the will, she did. Then, by faith, she received the healing for the emotional pain. Immediately after, she said, "I can hardly wait to get to the lawyer and tell him to drop the case."

This clearly shows how the Enemy gave her a plan of action and justified it with feelings of resentment in order to put her in bondage. Ananias and Sapphira, who were mentioned in the first chapter, were also inspired to a plan of action by the devil, and in their case, it resulted in physical death.

In both cases, they felt justified to carry out the devil's plan of action.

CHAPTER EIGHT

Freedom from Rejection and Rebellion

WHEN GOD CREATED US, He did so with precision and balance in mind. Aside from our physical existence, He has also created us with a complex and amazing psychological part. This is reflected in our personality, which is unique in every person. Like any other God-created function, the personality is intended to work in balance and in unity.

Every person has an introvert and an extrovert side to their personality. Most people are inclined to be either one or the other—they are outgoing and confident, or quiet and introspective. When these two functions are balanced, there is harmony in the personality. However, when there is over-emphasis on either side, the person becomes unbalanced, and great internal and external conflicts result.

Let us look at the following diagram to get a picture of how this balance works:

INTROVERT SIDE:

Input (listening)
Introspection
Reserve

EXTROVERT SIDE:

Output (speaking)
Expression
Confidence

THE GOD-CREATED BALANCE

Figure 8.1 - The Balance

Through our introvert side we receive input, we are thoughtful, and we are reserved. Through our extrovert side we give output, we are outgoing, and we are confident. A balanced person will maintain a comfortable level on both sides, with a bend towards one or the other, based upon the way God created him.

Maintaining this balance is essential to our mental well-being and, ultimately, to our spiritual well-being. Therefore, it is easy to conclude that the Enemy would want to try to throw us off balance.

Being thrown off balance can be done in two ways—by an internal experience of rejection, or by an outward expression of rebellion. Every one of us experiences rejection at some point in our lives. However, if we do not deal with it properly, it can then be a very destructive tool in the hand of the Enemy.

Whether a person is criticized or praised for what he does, the impact is always, "I am worth something because of my performance." Parents often make this mistake with their children: when their child does something that pleases them, they say, "Oh, you are a good boy/girl," but when the child does something displeasing, they say, "Oh, you are a bad boy/girl." This builds the false perception that "I am somebody because of *what I do*, and not because of *who I am*."

If a person experiences rejection, it will have the same effect on him whether the rejection is real or perceived. If we *believe* we have been rejected, even if we haven't, the same impact results. We withdraw and turn inward, and we begin to identify with the rejection and believe we really are no good. We then typically respond by rejecting ourselves in order to accommodate the feelings of rejection, and from there, we begin to fear rejection itself.

A poor self-image is a consequence of rejection: "I am no good. I look ugly. I cannot do anything right." A poor self-image is not only developed through rejection and criticism, but as you will see, it can also be developed through praise.

My Own Struggle

I grew up on praise. Physically, I grew up quickly, and by age twelve, I was the same height that I am now as an adult. In the small country school I attended, I could run the fastest, jump the highest, and could wrestle boys four years older than myself. I was also academically at the top of my class. As a result, I was praised all throughout my growing-up years.

My father died when I was twelve years old. Since I was the oldest boy in the family, I quit school and took over running the farm. Because I was big and strong, I was able to drive a team of horses at the threshing machine and carry many other adult responsibilities. People were amazed at what I was able to do. While my peers were out playing on the playground, I was doing a man's job. Because of this, I did not get much criticism, but I did get a lot of praise.

By the time I reached adulthood, my peers had caught up to me. I had finished growing, I wasn't becoming any stronger, and the things I did were no longer "out of the ordinary" for young men of my age. Some of my peers even began to surpass me, and so I stopped receiving the positive feedback I was accustomed to. I was no longer "exceptional," and my self-worth began to dissipate rapidly.

Over time, I came to feel like a "nobody" and also believed I was a nobody. I became very introverted. If there were more than two people in a room, I would not speak, even if they were my friends. I remained quiet so that people would not know how stupid I was (so I thought). I became totally controlled by what I thought people thought of me. I was frustrated with myself for being this way but was powerless to change.

Later, when I went to university, I took a particular course which required students to interact with each other and share their thoughts and feelings. I was the last one to muster up enough courage to speak, but after I had spoken a few times, the most talkative fellow in the group said to me in front of the class, "Henry, I envy you. You do not speak often, but when you do, we all listen because it is always worthwhile. When I talk, I just think out loud and then could bite my tongue afterward." At that moment, the longstanding lie was broken, and I began to recognize a truth: what I *assumed* people thought of me was *not* what they thought at all. More importantly, I allowed those assumed opinions of other people to govern me.

In my own experience, I was not aware of rebellion within me, but I did become deeply introverted. People were not able to get to know me because I felt I was not worthwhile to get to know. I didn't rebel because I knew if I did, there would be no praise given to me. In essence, the more worthless I felt, the more I withdrew, and the more paralyzed I became.

When a person is or feels rejected, he will initially withdraw and operate only from the introvert side of his personality. He will respond out of his feelings of inferiority, his fear of rejection, his poor self-image, and his depression—each adding a layer to the introvert side. As a result, the individual's psychological state is thrown into a state of imbalance, as seen below:

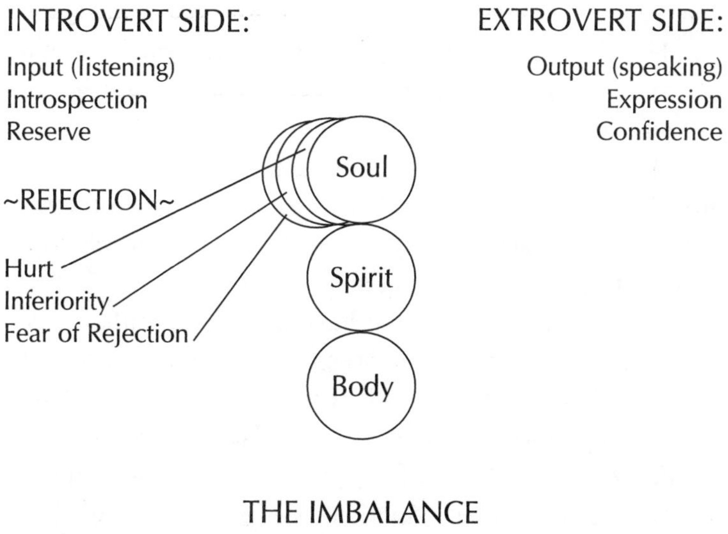

INTROVERT SIDE: EXTROVERT SIDE:

Input (listening)   Output (speaking)
Introspection   Expression
Reserve   Confidence

~REJECTION~

Hurt
Inferiority
Fear of Rejection

Soul

Spirit

Body

THE IMBALANCE

Figure 8.2 - The Imbalance

A Call for Help

If my finger is cut, there is an immediate "cry for help" signaled to the rest of my body. My body then sends the right number of white blood cells needed to help fight off any infection. Similarly, if someone is psychologically imbalanced, operating only from the introvert side of his personality, there is a "cry for help" to the extrovert side of his personality to help compensate for this imbalance.

This resulting response of this "call" to the extrovert side often manifests itself in rebellion. The Enemy convinces the rejected person that he is "just a doormat," suggesting that, instead of withdrawing, he should rebel and not allow others to walk all over him.

Rejection turns a person *inward*, but rebellion turns a person *outward*. Whereas rejection says, "I am not worth anything," rebellion says, "I am not going to be a doormat and let people walk all over me; I am somebody too, and I am going to live my own life." Figure 8.3 shows what this psychologically imbalanced state looks like.

As discussed earlier, when rejection is experienced, it is internalized in the form of "hurt." However, when the person's extrovert side tries to compensate through rebellion, "anger" is expressed, adding another layer.

On the introvert side, we have a layer of "inferiority." When this inferiority is expressed on the extrovert side through rebellion, the individual lashes out with an expression of "superiority." Now *he* treats *others* like "doormats"! Similarly, when a "fear of rejection" is expressed through the extrovert side, the individual will protect himself from being wounded again by first "rejecting others." With this, we add yet another layer to this terrible imbalance.

As long as the person is on the "rejection side" of introversion, he will remain passive, but when he moves into the "rebellion side" of extroversion, he will likely lash out against those he sees as the oppressors. Even if his perception is not true, his "colored-glasses" will make him interpret situations from a tainted view. And if he rebels, he becomes vulnerable to witchcraft. As Samuel said to King Saul in 1 Samuel 15:23a, *"For rebellion is as the sin of witchcraft, and stubbornness is as iniquity and idolatry."* By getting a person to become rebellious and stubborn, the Enemy has gained an effective open door.

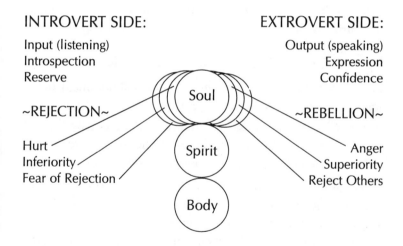

INTROVERT SIDE:

Input (listening)
Introspection
Reserve

~REJECTION~

Hurt
Inferiority
Fear of Rejection

EXTROVERT SIDE:

Output (speaking)
Expression
Confidence

~REBELLION~

Anger
Superiority
Reject Others

Soul

Spirit

Body

THE IMBALANCE

Figure 8.3 - Personality in Conflict

Instead of solving his problem, the person who lives out of rebellion now has a double problem—rejection *and* rebellion. On the one hand, the person feels rejected and inferior, on the other hand, he lashes out destructively to prove to himself that he is a "somebody." But afterward, he is left with feelings of more rejection and inferiority. The person becomes totally helpless to maintain the balance that God created for him. People are usually not aware of the switch from rejection to rebellion, and it is usually through counseling that they become aware of it.

When a person stays in rejection and never switches to rebellion, he becomes bound up and dysfunctional. He is not free to function and enjoy life, and God cannot use him because he continues to believe lies about himself. If the person does rebel, he still feels rejection deep inside, and it is confusing to him because he switches back and forth. He leans to the introvert side, but then catapults to the extrovert side.

Different Responses in Different People

A classroom bully feels inferior and cannot stand being ignored. If he behaves well, he is generally left alone, but being left alone is more difficult for him to handle than to receive negative responses. Therefore, he misbehaves to get attention and believes that the negative attention is better than no attention at all.

One high school teacher on my staff was a brilliant conversationalist and was always the centre of attention in the staff room. I'd look at him and think he had "the world by the tail." One day, he came to me for counseling and said, "I brag to the point of lying so that people will think that I am somebody, because I really feel like I am a nobody." He became an extrovert to compensate for his fear of rejection.

We should never try to deal with our psychological imbalance through our soul, but through our spirit. Trying to help people build up their souls is the greatest failure of modern psychology. The Enemy wants us to strengthen the soul in order to destroy us further. In contrast to this, God wants the expression of the soul to be subservient to that of the spirit. He wants us to see ourselves and our circumstances through *His* eyes, which is seeing things through our spirit.

How do we minister to imbalanced people like this? We help them understand that rejection and rebellion are sins and that they both need to be confessed. Though it is an internal response, receiving rejection is still sin because the person is believing the Enemy's lies and is not believing what God says about him. Rebellion is outward and obvious sin, but its root is the same as rejection—at the heart of rebellion there is a lie believed. Whenever we believe the Enemy's lies, we are sinning against God.

We now see how important it is to differentiate between the approaches of God and that of Satan. The Enemy comes through the soul and influences our perspective, trying to control us, whereas God comes directly through the spirit with the truth that sets us free (John 8:32).

CHAPTER NINE

God Actually Uses the Enemy

Becoming an Overcomer

IT IS ESSENTIAL THAT we understand that God in His love uses the Enemy to accomplish great things in His children. If we fail to recognize this truth, suffering and grief will make no sense and will seem to have no purpose. My heart is that people will embrace and understand that the things God allows the devil to bring to us are really loving lessons from His hand.

From the moment we become saved, God could insulate us from the devil, but He doesn't. Without opposition in our lives, there would be little or no growth. A coach can teach all the skills of a certain sport, but unless the players play against live opponents, they will never become champions. God is looking for overcomers. How could we become overcomers unless we had something to overcome? Therefore, He uses the devil as an opponent for our practice.

Pruning Shears

I am the true vine, my Father is the husbandman, Every branch in me that beareth not fruit, he taketh away, and every branch that beareth fruit, he purgeth that it may bring forth more fruit (John 15: 1-2).

Jesus is the vine, and we are the branches (John 15:5). The vine produces the fruit. The branch only bears it. When the Gardener wants the branches to bear more fruit, He uses the pruning shears to cut away anything that hinders growth. I believe the devil is often the pruning shears that God uses to trim and cut. Oh, how it hurts sometimes! Pruning shears in the hands of a maniac are dangerous, but in the hands of a loving Father, they are a totally safe and good thing.

Punishment or Chastisement

A distraught single mom came to see me. Her only son, who was seventeen, had run away from home. She was convinced that God was punishing her for her past sins. I told her that God would not be punishing her for her past sins because Jesus had paid for those, but that God might be chastising her. She could not understand that. In her mind, chastisement was equal to punishment. I consulted a dictionary and proceeded to read to her the definitions of the word "chastisement." There are three basic meanings of the word "chastisement":[2]

1. *Punishment with the view of improvement.* This is what we would define as child training.

2. *Refinement.* God uses the Enemy as the refiner's fire, bringing the dross and impurities to the surface of the gold. These are skimmed off; more heat is then applied, and still more dross comes to the surface. This is

repeated until the gold is pure. At what point does the refiner know when the gold is pure? When he can see his own reflection in the gold, he knows. What an awesome picture of God's intention to have us reflect Him to others. Therefore, we should rejoice when we are being refined.

Refining in the Life of Rees Howell

Rees Howell was a mighty intercessor on behalf of the people and leadership of Great Britain during the dark days of World War II. He was a humble man of God, but God desired to work an even greater humility in his life by refining him. One day, the Lord spoke clearly to him: "When you pray, I do not want you to have your head covered." Thus, when he was by himself in prayer, Howell would remove his hat. Then God told him that he must always be in an attitude of prayer, even in public; therefore Howell was never to wear his hat. Now, during that particular time in England, you would never see a man in public without his hat. And so, to not wear one was very humbling for Howell. To make matters worse, every time he went to leave his house, his mother would be standing at the door with his hat in her hands because she did not want him to be an outcast. Howell did not want to offend his mother, but he wanted to obey God. He therefore did not wear his hat. God uses these kinds of refining trials to expose the self-centredness in our lives that hinders us from being as useful to Him as He desires.

3. *Temper.* This is the third meaning of "chastisement." If we take a piece of steel, wind it up in the form of a spring, stretch it, and then let go, the steel remains stretched because it has not been tempered. Tempering

is a process of heating the metal to high temperatures and then cooling it rapidly. This strengthens and hardens the steel. When a tempered spring is stretched and then let go, it immediately retracts to its former position. Nothing can pull it out of shape. Praise God that He is in the business of tempering us, that no matter what we go through, nothing can pull us out of shape.

Watchspring or Horseshoe?

Tempering steel increases the value of the steel. If a person buys $10 worth of steel and heats and shapes it into five horseshoes, it would be valued at about $25. If that same piece of steel is made into sewing needles, it could be worth as much as $250. The same piece of steel being made into penknife blades would yield as much as $2500. However, if that piece of steel was made into watchsprings, through the tempering process, the value would increase to $250,000.

We may grumble and complain under God's tempering and remain only as a horseshoe, or we can yield and surrender to God and allow Him to make us into a watchspring.

Often God allows the Enemy to do the tempering, as He allowed the devil to "sift" Peter. Sometimes God even sets up the devil, as He did in the case of Job, to mature Job to sonship.

In the life of Jesus, we have an example of this stability. Whether the crowd wanted to crown Him as King, or whether they called for His death, Jesus remained unaffected and focused on His Father.

The Surrendered Life

As we realize that God is who He says He is, we will be able to rest and let Him do the work. This is the first step to "moving out in faith." When we surrender our lives to God, we are, in essence, saying to Him, "God, I take my hands off my life, and I ask You to take full responsibility for running it." Many people are taught to take this first step, but often in the midst of circumstances, they step backward and take control again because they aren't entirely sure that God will be there to take responsibility.

The second step to moving out in faith is to *believe* that God has now taken responsibility. If everything goes wrong the next day and things get worse, the devil will be there to say, "See, it didn't work!" You can in faith say, "God I gave You my life, I surrendered myself to You, and I know You want to be Lord of my life. Therefore, I know You have taken over the responsibility for my life. You are still in control of what is happening now, and You are going to bring me through it."

In the difficult circumstances you are going through, it is important to reaffirm the truth that you have taken your hands off your life and have given it to God to take care of. Just because things may go wrong, it is no indication that God didn't take responsibility. This is the point where faith comes in—believing and knowing that God is at the helm.

What to Pray

It is crucial to realize that often when we pray to God for things for ourselves, we are usually assuming we know what is good for us. But, like little children, we really do not know. Some of the best things I have given to my children were spankings when they needed them. Of course, they did not think so at the time, but now they tell my wife and me how they appreciated our consistency in discipline.

When we pray, we want to always leave ourselves open to what God knows to be best for our lives. Ephesians 3:20 says,

God is able *"to do exceedingly abundantly above all that we ask or think, according to the power that worketh in us."*

Sometimes, in being specific with our requests, we limit God. I am not saying we should not be specific, but what *we* specifically want or desire may be in conflict with what *God* wants for us. When our circumstances conflict with our requests, and we react negatively to them, we may entirely miss what God desired to accomplish through those circumstances.

Like a good shepherd, God takes us through the valleys and permits trying circumstances to refine us. After we have come through the trying times and look back, like the Psalmist we may say,

> *Before I was afflicted I went astray: but now I have kept thy word.... It is good for me that I have been afflicted; that I might learn thy statutes* (Psalm 119:67,71).

Christ learned obedience through the things He suffered. God's Son emptied Himself, took the form of a man, and walked on this earth without sin. Even though He went through the same temptations as we do now, and though He endured the same sufferings to learn obedience, He did not sin. If Christ did all this, then surely there is no shortcut for us.

Paul and the Thorn in the Flesh

> *And lest I should be exalted above measure through the abundance of the revelations, there was given to me a thorn in the flesh, the messenger of Satan to buffet me, lest I should be exalted above measure. For this thing I besought the Lord thrice, that it might depart from me. And he said unto me, My grace is sufficient for thee: for my strength is made perfect in weakness. Most gladly therefore will I glory in my*

infirmities, that the power of Christ may rest upon me. Therefore I take pleasure in infirmities, in reproaches, in necessities, in persecutions, in distresses for Christ's sake: for when I am weak, then am I strong (2 Corinthians 12:7-10).

Paul speaks here of the thorn in his flesh. There are two reasons why God would allow this thorn in Paul's life. The first reason is that God had revealed so much to Paul, he was in danger of becoming proud. Paul could be tempted to think, "I must be very special and important, considering God has revealed so much to me." The second reason was to create a need in Paul for the grace of God:

There was given to me... [Who gave it? God did.] *the messenger of Satan* [a demon] *to buffet me* [to hit blow upon blow]*, lest I be exalted above measure.*

This demon was given to Paul to protect him from falling into pride and maybe even becoming useless for the Kingdom of God. Paul recognized this himself: *"...lest that by any means, when I have preached to others, I myself should be a castaway"* (1 Corinthians 9:27).

"Make Me More Christ-Like"

In 1981, I prayed the prayer, "Lord, do anything in my life, but make me more Christ-like." Later, when I shared this with the staff at Christian Enrichment Family Camp, one of them said, "I would be too scared to do that." I replied, "I'm not scared to pray in this manner because I know my Father."

Shortly after I had prayed that prayer, we were trenching a sewer line across the yard of our camp. We crossed an old existing line, a trench that had been dug about twelve years

132

prior. There were water, sewer, and telephone lines that we tried to avoid, but unfortunately, we cut through all the pipes, as well as the telephone line. I went into town to get the fittings to repair it while my son Jake, who was nineteen years old, began to clear dirt from the pipes so we could fix them.

On my way back from town, I was met by one of our camp vehicles. There had been an accident; the trench had caved in, and my son had been buried up to his neck. He was lying on a board in the back of the van, and they were going to meet the ambulance which was on its way.

Initially, this incident did not hit me that hard. I went to the hospital with him, and they found that his right shoulder and four ribs were broken. He was sent to a larger hospital for an operation on his shoulder. They did not operate however, because they were afraid of causing more damage by cutting through the muscles. Two days later, they released him from the hospital. The doctor thought he was ready to go.

Jake was in agony at home. The next day, he developed such pain in his left shoulder, he could not feel the pain from his broken one. He could hardly move. We telephoned the doctor who said Jake was bruised badly and it would take some time to heal. On the fifth morning after his discharge from the hospital, Jake collapsed and struggled for breath. The staff nurse immediately phoned the ambulance. Wouldn't you know, the ambulance arrived at the same time the cement truck did, and the cement truck operator had already begun dumping the cement. So, while the ambulance took my son, I had to trowel cement. This was very traumatic for me, having to work with cement while my son was on the verge of death.

After I helped level out the cement to the point that the other person could handle it, a nurse from the local hospital telephoned and said that things looked serious. They had given him a stimulant and were now rushing him to a larger hospital sixty miles away for exploratory surgery. My wife and I left immediately to meet them there.

It was during that sixty mile drive that I went through what I call a "Gethsemane experience." I knew what I had prayed earlier. I therefore had no assurance that God was not going to take Jake home. Knowing that my son was in critical condition, I struggled inwardly. I identified with Abraham when he was asked to offer up Isaac. But I knew that even if Jake died, it would be a graduation for my son because he loved the Lord. But was I willing to give him up? My wife wanted to talk to me, but I couldn't talk; the inner turmoil was so intense. After a time, I chose to release him into God's hands. I thanked God that He had entrusted him into our care for twenty years, and told Him I was releasing him back into God's care. At that moment, *"the peace that passes all understanding"* (Philippians 4:7) came over me.

When we walked into the hospital, a chaplain friend of mine met us at the door. He informed us that Jake's red blood count was only 4.5 (normal levels are around 16-18). The oxygen-carrying capacity of Jake's blood was almost non-existent. They had given Jake three pints of blood already and had just taken him to the operating room. We were taken to a room where we waited one and a half hours before the doctor came to see us. Amazingly, I had perfect peace during that time. Yes, there was concern, but there was no battle. The battle had been won.

Surgery revealed that Jake's spleen had been crushed and that he had been bleeding internally for seven days. This was the cause of the immense pain he had been experiencing. The doctors ended up removing his crushed spleen; my son recovered, and to this day, he is still doing well.

Throughout this event, God "hits many birds with one stone." Not only was He teaching me a great lesson, but He did a deep work in my son's life during his stay in the hospital as well. Jake was such a go-getter. Before the accident, we would discuss our tasks and plans for the day, and he would impatiently say, "Well, Dad, let's get going and not just talk about it." It was in that hospital where he learned patience. The doctor would tell him that in three days he could go home. However, when the three days were up, he told him he would have to stay another three days, and then another three days. Finally, Jake learned to rest, knowing that God's timetable was trustworthy. He said to me, "I don't even ask the doctor anymore because I know in God's time I'll be out."

Jake also learned that many people cared about him, and in this, he learned compassion. "If this had happened to someone else," he said, " I wouldn't have cared for them as much as people have cared for me." Later, his cousin was in a serious car accident and was in a coma for weeks. Because of his own suffering, Jake was able to empathize with the family and others who were in distress.

Later that same summer, I shared this testimony at our camp. A year later, a lady came in for counseling and told me that she had been there at the camp and had heard my testimony. She said, "I could not receive it; I thought it was too harsh." However, later that year, the economy took a sharp downturn, interest rates soared to 22 percent, and her husband, who was a self-employed electrician, couldn't get any work. They were required to sell their beautiful home in a district where they had many friends, and they had to buy a much cheaper home in a poor district where they had no friends. She was really struggling. One day, she talked to a lady who had come to camp with her the previous summer. Her friend said, "You should listen to the tapes I bought of the lessons Henry taught last summer." The woman listened to the tapes, and finally, the message ministered life to her because she was in *need* of those truths. Unless we are aware of our need of a certain truth, we may hear the truth, but it will not be a revelation to us.

Knowing How to Stop

When I was a child, there were not many cars around in the country, and no cars in our district. We all drove with horses. So, when my uncle bought a car, he needed to know how to operate that car. First, he needed to know how to start it (and back in those days it wasn't simply just turning a key). He had to put the spark in just the right place and crank it by hand. If the spark was not at the right place, it could kick his arm out as the engine backfired. Second, my uncle needed to know how to drive that car, and third, he needed to know how to stop that car. As the person from whom he bought the car explained all these things to him, my uncle neglected to remember the part about stopping. It did not seem important to him at that time, since the car was not moving yet. So, he got the car started and drove it to our farm, but when he got there, he did not know how to stop. I remember him driving through our fence and driving around and around our house. If somebody had told him *then* how to stop the car, it would have registered because the need for that truth was much stronger at that moment.

We don't always recognize what God wants to reveal to us for our benefit and His Glory, and so we grumble about the trials we go through. We then ask God to get us out of the trial and don't see that God wants to reveal to us our need to mature.

When Paul besought the Lord three times, asking that the thorn might depart from him, the Lord answered, *"My grace is sufficient for thee, for my strength is made perfect in weakness"* (2 Corinthians 12:9). What a deep truth this is! Often, Christians pray that God will strengthen them so they can endure their problem. God does not want to strengthen our flesh. He allowed the devil to make Paul aware of his weakness and of his inability to handle the onslaught of the Enemy, to make him a candidate for God's unlimited strength. When Paul grasped this truth, he exclaimed, *"Most gladly therefore, will I rather glory in my infirmities, that the power of Christ may rest upon me"* (2 Corinthians 12:9). That is exchanged strength—God's strength in exchange for our weakness.

> ***But they that wait upon the Lord shall renew their strength****; they shall mount up with wings as eagles; they shall run, and not be weary; and they shall walk, and not faint* [emphasis mine] (Isaiah 40:31).

The Hebrew word here, for the word "renew," could be better translated as "exchange," for it implies that something must be given in order to receive. For us to experience God's strength, we have to be first made aware of our utter weakness: *"I will rather glory in my infirmities...."* We tend to grumble about our weaknesses and shortcomings. But Paul said, *"I even take pleasure in infirmities, in reproaches, in necessities, in persecution, in distresses for Christ's sake"* (2 Corinthians 12:9,10). When God allowed this demon to work in Paul, it was for Christ's sake. God desires that we become as dependent upon Christ, as Christ was upon His Father.

> *But He giveth more grace.... God resisteth the proud... submit yourselves therefore to God. Resist the devil and he will flee from you* (James 4:6,7).

Job: The Study of Mature Sonship

The study of the book of Job provides one of the most exciting insights into how God uses the devil to accomplish a far greater purpose in the lives of His children.

The book of Job is the oldest book in the Bible, and God, through the life of Job, clearly shows us His ultimate purpose for every person. God's purpose in every one of us is to make us Christ-like, totally yielded and committed to Christ, as Christ was committed to His Father.

If Job had just resisted the devil when God allowed him to attack, Job would have done what many Christians do today—he would have tried to defeat the devil. In doing this, Job would have missed the great plan that God had intended for him, and he would not have matured toward sonship.

I believe we always have to resist the devil's lies. When he gives us thoughts and feelings that are not based on truth, we need to recognize his devices and resist him. However, when God *permits* the devil to come at us through people or circumstances that we cannot control, we need to *submit* to God and *choose* to see our situation as an opportunity for growth. God will use the devil to expose to us where the flesh is still active, or to reveal God to us in a far greater way than we have known, as He did to Job. This is shown in Job's statement, *"I have heard of thee by the hearing of the ear: but now my eye seeth thee"* (Job 42:5).

Stephen Kaung, compiler of many of Watchman Nee's teachings, drew some insightful analogies in his own book, *The Splendor of His Ways—Seeing the Lord's End in Job*. This "end" was that Job would be able to inherit the double blessing due the firstborn son at maturity—the final goal of full sonship.[3] Grasping this is key to putting God's use of the devil into perspective, for if our eyes do not see what God's final purpose is, then we will be tempted to resist or shorten God's dealings in our lives and ultimately miss the greater work at hand.

An intriguing and deeper truth can be seen in the characters of Job's three "friends" and the young Elihu. Each character represents trying to grasp God and His ways through the intellect, the emotions, the will, and the human spirit.

Eliphaz is an example of trying to understand God through the emotions. He drew his arguments from intangibles and from what he *felt* and *experienced*. His basis in approaching Job came largely from a supernatural experience, though we are not told it was from God. We can never understand God through the emotions. If we try, we become susceptible to accepting a counterfeit, as we know the devil will work through feelings. Job's response was also emotional.

Bildad represents trying to understand God through intellect and logic. We see that he drew his arguments from tradition or tangible things that he could understand and prove (Job 8). His was the theology of cause and effect. Though we try, the mind cannot discern a spiritual problem: *"Canst thou by searching find out God?"* (Job 11:7a).

Zophar, was the eldest of the four and the most impatient. He was blunt, his accusations direct. He represents the will and dogmatism. Zophar gave his opinion strongly yet provided little in the way of backing it up. He exhorted Job to repent, *"and the days of comfort will come to you"* (Job 11:13-19). Like many Christians, Zophar oversimplified truth but neglected the spirit of the matter.

Elihu, the youngest of the four, represented the human spirit. He was humble and waited until all the men had finished, and then with youthful passion, he began to speak of the spirit of man. Angered by both Job's defense of himself and by the condemnation levied by Job's friends, Elihu, whose name means, "Who is your God?" spoke in God's defense by the Spirit.

As long as the men were trying to understand God and His ways by the soul engaging the intellect, emotions, and will, God was silent. They did not realize God's intention because, through the soul, we are incapable of understanding God's ways. It was only after the soul was quieted and when they engaged the spirit that God spoke into the matter.

In the end portion of the book of Job, God takes the centre position, and we hear of His grandeur and awesomeness, leaving no doubt in our minds that He has been fully in control of the entire drama, having orchestrated it Himself. The workings of the devil set the stage for God to reveal Himself. Job had asked many questions of God, and then fell silent. God did not answer Job's questions, but He asked many of His own questions, to which Job had no answer:

> *Where wast thou when I laid the foundations of the earth? declare, if thou hast understanding.... Where is the way where light dwelleth? and as for darkness, where is the place thereof.... By what way is the light parted, which scattereth the east wind upon the earth.... Shall he that contendeth with the Almighty instruct him? He that reproveth God, let him answer it* (Job 38:4,19,24; 40:2).

Each question lowered Job's confidence in himself, and when God was finished, Job answered God by saying,

> *I know that thou canst do everything, and that no thought can be withholden from thee. Who is he that hideth counsel without knowledge? Therefore have I uttered that I understood not; things too wonderful*

*for me, which I knew not.... I have heard of thee by the
hearing of the ear: but now mine eye seeth thee.
Wherefore I abhor myself, and repent in dust and
ashes* (Job 42:2-3,5-6).

Four Levels of Maturity

God's purpose in allowing the Enemy to influence our lives
is to bring us into spiritual maturity. The devil is unable to do
what he wants; he can do only what God allows him to do.

The first level on the way towards maturity is childhood.
The Apostle Paul challenged the Corinthians, telling them
they were still babes. He thus still had to give them only spiritual "milk" because they were unable to digest spiritual
"meat" (1 Corinthians 3:2). Paul expected them to have
already matured beyond infancy. We begin our Christian walk
by *accepting Christ as our Saviour.* That is the infancy of our
walk. Jesus, however, wants us to move beyond our infancy;
He wants to be more than just our Saviour.

Adolescence is the second level in Christian develop-
ment; it is the time when we *accept Christ as Lord.* Job had
done this. He was obedient to God as Lord, which is why God
spoke highly of him:

*And the LORD said unto Satan, Hast thou considered
my servant Job, that there is none like him in the earth,
a perfect man, one that escheweth evil? And still hold-
eth fast his integrity, although thou movest me against
him, to destroy him without cause* (Job 2:3).

I believe that Job was in an adolescent stage at the beginning of the book. Within that adolescent stage, he was perfect,
but God wasn't satisfied with where Job was. He wanted to
bring Job into a deeper maturity.

If a five year old draws a picture, no matter how bizarre or meaningless it appears, the mother will proudly pin it on the fridge. We may look at that picture and not have a clue of what it is supposed to be. Nevertheless, it is a perfect picture for a five-year-old. However, if at age twenty, the child is still drawing that same kind of picture, the mother would be ashamed and would not display it. God wants us to grow up into spiritual maturity.

The third stage towards spiritual maturity is friendship:

Ye are my friends if ye do whatsoever I command you. Henceforth I call you not servants; for the servant knoweth not what his lord doeth: but I have called you friends; for all things that I have heard of my Father I have made known unto you (John 15:14-15).

Abraham was called a friend of God. When he hosted the heavenly visitors, the Lord said, *"Shall I hide from Abraham the thing which I do"* (Genesis 18:17). In this situation in Genesis, it really wasn't any of Abraham's business what God was going to do to the city of Sodom, but because of God's friendship with Abraham, God chose to share His plan with him.

When we *accept Christ as our life*, we have reached the final stage of maturity:

I am crucified with Christ: nevertheless I live; yet not I, but Christ liveth in me: and the life which I now live in the flesh I live by faith of the Son of God, who loved me, and gave himself for me (Galatians 2:20).

We cannot live the Christian life in our own strength. We'll always fail if we try, but we can depend on Christ to live it through us. It is only God that can make a demon leave; we can command him, but it is God that makes him go. If God removes the demon before He has achieved His purpose in us, then we have suffered in vain. If you see a man who can't swim fall into deep water, and you have nothing to throw to him, the only option you have is to jump in and try to save his life. If you jump in right away while he is still fighting and screaming for help, he will grab you and pull you down, and you will both drown. However, if you wait until he is totally exhausted and has no strength left, you can then swiftly jump in and save his life. In the same manner, God will wait until all our strength and independence is gone before stepping in.

"What Would I Do Without You?"

Julie, a young lady who had many demonic problems, was set free from one demon after another. However, towards the end of her deliverance, one particular demon refused to go. Each time she came to see me, she hoped to be set free from this last demon. The demon just sneered, "I've got power, and you won't get me out." I used all the commands and Scriptures that made the other ones go, and I was perplexed as to why this one could stay so long. One day, Julie came to a point of surrender and was able to say to God, "In Your time." That decision was a big step forward. She chose to trust that God would release the demon from her, and she would not insist on the timing. One day, God asked a question of her: "Julie, if I would never set you free and would never bless you again, would you still love Me and follow Me?" This was a very hard question because the demon was threatening her life. She contemplated it for a while, and then she said to God, "What would I do without you? Even if You never set me free and never bless me again, I will still love You and follow You."

143

I did not know about this conversation between her and God, and so, that night I commanded the demon to leave, just as I had done many times before. All of sudden her arms flung wide, her eyes sprung wide open, and she was free! God allowed her a prolonged deliverance in order to draw her to Himself in a deeper and more committed way.

When God brought Job to the attention of the devil, the devil said, "Does Job serve you for nothing?" The devil, in effect, was saying to God, "God, in order to get people to follow You, You have to stoop to the same methods I use. You bless Job and protect him, and that is why he follows you" (Job 1:9-10). The devil was implying that God bribed Job to follow him, just as the devil does to his followers. But through Job's unwavering commitment, the devil was silenced. In the case of Julie, I saw that God waited until He knew that she was ready to follow Him for nothing, thus silencing the devil in her life.

The End of the Lord: His Final Purpose in Us

> *Behold, we count them happy which endure. Ye have heard of the patience of Job, and have seen the **end** of the Lord; that the Lord is very pitiful, and of tender mercy* [emphasis mine] (James 5:11).

The "end of the Lord" is the key to the book of Job. The Lord had an end or final purpose for Job, and He has the same purpose for our lives. God's purpose for allowing the devil to work was to perfect Job's faith and knowledge of God. Finally, the end or the purpose is seen—as Job said, *"I have heard of thee by the hearing of the ear: but now mine eye seeth thee"* (Job 42:5).

God blesses us when He gives us things, but when He takes things away, it can become an even greater blessing:

*Blessed be the God and Father of our Lord Jesus Christ, which according to his abundant mercy hath begotten us again unto a lively hope by the resurrection of Jesus Christ from the dead, To an inheritance incorruptible, and undefiled, and that fadeth not away, reserved in heaven for you, Who are kept by the power of God through faith unto salvation ready to be revealed in the last time. Wherein ye greatly rejoice, though now for a season, if need be, ye are in heaviness through manifold temptations: **That the trial of your faith, being much more precious than of gold that perisheth**, though it be tried with fire, might be found unto praise and honour and glory at the appearing of Jesus Christ: Whom having not seen, ye love; in whom, though now ye see him not, yet believing, ye rejoice with joy unspeakable and full of glory: receiving the **end of your faith**, even the salvation of your souls* [emphasis mine] (1 Peter 1:3-9).

This is the final and highest purpose of our faith, the salvation of our souls, having come through the trial of our faith.

Joseph: From Prison to Prime Minister

Another example of how God uses the devil to perfect and mature His children can be found in the life of Joseph. Joseph's brothers, inspired by the devil through jealousy, captured him and sold him as a slave. It was the devil-inspired Potiphar's wife who accused him falsely and was instrumental in having him imprisoned. We do not know about Joseph's inner struggle during those thirteen years, but it seems clear that he must have chosen to see the hand of God in each situation.

At the end, when Joseph made himself known to his brothers, he said, *"ye thought evil against me; but God meant it unto good...* (Genesis 50:20). The Enemy would have wanted Joseph to become bitter and resentful, and his brothers and Potiphar's wife produced the occasions for Joseph to become justified in his mind towards bitterness and resentment. But because Joseph chose not to give into the resentment the Enemy imposed, he was able to be prepared as an instrument of righteousness.

Overnight, Joseph was promoted from prisoner to prime minister and, yet, the instant success didn't destroy him. This shows us how valuable those thirteen years of preparation had been.

Overcoming the Devil

We tend to think that Jesus only overcame the devil on the cross, however, He defeated the devil every day of His life. While we can depend on the fact that Christ defeated the Enemy on the cross, we, too, have to thwart the devil's daily attempts to put us into bondage.

The devil's attacks are not always openly negative. The temptations of Jesus in the wilderness were positive on the surface, and the devil will even tempt us to "do good," to keep us from God's perfect and best will for our lives.

In the story of Saul, God told Saul to destroy some animals. The devil, however, succeeded in getting Saul to be disobedient by suggesting to Saul he should choose not to destroy the animals, *"in order to sacrifice* [them] *to the Lord."* instead (1 Samuel 15:15). A temptation of this sort is very subtle—how could God be displeased if the animals were sacrificed to Him? God, though, was displeased, and the Kingdom was taken from Saul.

The story of King David is another clear example. From the time he was anointed to be king, David may have anticipated that God would just enable him to be a good king. It probably was a shock to him that God enrolled him in the University of "Hard Knocks." Instead, his life was constantly in danger by the demon-inspired Saul, and God permitted it, or even designed it, in order to prepare David as a vessel that He could use.

The Task or the Person?

The person is more important than the task. God uses tasks to perfect the person.

Often, we are so task-oriented and think that if we do God's task, that is the highest goal we can reach. God's goal for us is much higher than the task. He can always get someone else to do the task He has in mind. God is more interested in shaping us into the people He intended us to be: *"we are the clay, and thou our potter"* (Isaiah 64:8).

> *...well done, thou good and faithful servant: thou hast been faithful over a few things, I will set thee ruler over many things. Enter thou into the joy of thy lord* (Matthew 25:21,23).

In the above Scripture about "The Parable of the Talents," The master spoke the same words to both the servant who made five talents, and to the one who made two talents: *"Well, done, thou good and faithful servant...."* So, in effect, the Master (God) doesn't reward quantity, but faithfulness. God is preparing us for eternity. Often we are so time-conscious and temporal-minded, we are tempted to grumble and complain, "Why do we have to go through the sufferings when we are trying to do God's will here on earth?" We need God's eternal vision and an understanding of His *end purpose.*

147

My Own Testimony

In 1975, God gave me a heart-vision to teach in a Bible College. I wanted to be in a place where I would be able to share with people from different churches the life-changing truths that God had revealed to me, in the hopes that these truths might bear fruit in other people and in other churches. I thought I was ready and started applying to various Bible Colleges. I was very confident of God's leading, so I quit my job as the counselor in a high school in March of 1975.

Previously, I had made Paul's prayer my own. Philippians 3:10 says,

That I might know him, and the power of his resurrection and the fellowship of his sufferings, being made conformable unto his death.

I had seen many people delivered from demonic oppression and thus released into freedom in Christ; I wanted to see more of God's power as He set people free. Thus, my emphasis in that verse was on the *"power of his resurrection,"* but I didn't realize that I had no idea what that phrase meant. The word "resurrection" had not yet come alive to me. I always prayed the whole verse, but did not focus on the last part of the verse, *"the fellowship of his suffering, being made conformable unto his death."* God's emphasis, as I have discovered, was on this latter part of the verse, and I became aware that the latter part has to be experienced *first*, before we can receive the power of the resurrection. My thought was, "If I simply had more power, more demons would be cast out and more people would be set free." Resurrection, however, means that something that is alive has to die first before it can receive new life—namely, resurrection life. Thus, God proceeded to bring that death into my life.

It was disappointing to get no response from the Bible Colleges I had applied to. None of them even acknowledged they had received my application. I did not know why God was keeping the door closed, especially since He had given me the vision to teach in a Bible College. Because He kept the doors closed, I applied to different school divisions, confident that since I had experience and the academic training in a number of areas, I would certainly get a job again. But even the school divisions were silent.

By the end of June, I still had no response. One day, while praying about what to do, it came to me to telephone one particular school division and inquire. I spoke with the superintendent, and when I told him who I was, he said, "I've got your application right here on my desk, and I am very interested in you." He invited me to come for an interview. He offered me two positions. One was in town, the other in a two-room country village school. I had found out by now that he was a Christian and so I said, "I do not want to choose what *I* want; I trust that God will guide you to put me where God wants me." He said, "That's easy, I'll put you in the country school. Later, we can move you to town."

For years, I had taught in one and two-room country schools, and I had very positive and fond memories of those years. I found myself looking forward to getting back into the family-type setting of the rural school.

I bought an old house on eight acres of land. I spent the whole summer, for ten to twelve hours a day, renovating that house. Our children loved it, and they attended a different two-room school in the district we lived in. They really enjoyed their school life.

The students in my new classroom cooperated, and I came to love them, although there were quite a few low-achievers. Things were going well.

It was also at this time that I met the young pastor in the rural church close to us. When I shared with him about deliverance, it was quite new to him, but he was interested, and he said, "Would you be willing to teach about this on Wednesday nights?" I was more than willing to do that. I shared many of the concepts that are in this book. The farmers in the area came out every Wednesday night, even though it was in the middle of harvest time. It was rewarding to see their interest.

Everything was going fine until the end of October. One morning, I walked into the classroom, and most of the students had turned against me. I did not understand what had hit me! Before, they had been very cooperative, and now they argued about any assignment I gave them. They were disrespectful to the point of being rude. I had never experienced this type of behaviour and attitude in any students before! Every day I had to drag myself to school because I found it so hard to have this disrespect. I tried every technique that had worked before in other classes; now, none of them worked.

For the first time in my life, I understood the meaning of the verse I had known by memory for years. Jesus says in John 15:5, *"Without me you can do nothing."* Those had been mere words to me before, but now they became reality. I knew, that I knew, that I *knew*, that I couldn't solve this problem. Up until this time, I had been successful. Now, I saw myself as a total failure.

The superintendent would come to the school and say, "What's happening in this school?" I would ask him what he meant. He said, "I am getting anonymous phone calls from parents who are accusing you and the school of things." The accusations were false, and I knew then that the parents had turned against me, as well as the kids.

Suddenly, the church where I had shared every Wednesday night for the previous eight weeks closed the door without any explanation. I gathered that some influential person was objecting to my teaching. Without any forewarning, I felt ostracized. I really began to identify with Job, who had calamity upon calamity reported to him, with no recovery time in between. Like Job, I was stripped of everything I could depend on. In my case, the students had turned against me without warning, the parents had turned against me, and the church had turned against me. The fourth thing that happened occurred shortly afterward. I was playing soccer with the boys at school, and one of them ran into me with his shoulder, causing me excruciating pain. It was probably broken ribs. I was so high on believing in God's healing at that time that I thought I didn't need to go to the doctor; I believed God would just heal me. There was no improvement week after week, and I knew I wasn't healing. I had really come to the end of myself.

When I had applied to teach in Bible Colleges, I thought I was ready to work for God. Now I realized that God was showing me that without Him, I could do *nothing*. But even when I thought I had now learned the lesson that God had to strip me before He could use me, still nothing changed in my circumstances.

I began to see how my struggle was affecting my own children. They saw my unhappiness and wondered what they had done wrong. Towards the end of November, I finally felt I had no choice but to resign from the school, acknowledging that I was a failure.

In that particular district, if you resigned by the end of November, it wasn't held against you, and you would be able to assume another post. I talked with the superintendent, but he didn't want to accept my resignation. He reasoned that I hadn't lost control of the class. I told him that the children would learn more under a teacher they would cooperate with. He encouraged me to stay.

I agreed to stay and dragged on until the middle of December. By then, I felt that I could not function any longer.

I went to see the superintendent again on a Saturday, and after further discussion, he finally accepted my resignation, saying I needed to hand in my written resignation by Monday after school, "unless you change your mind." I thought that there was not much chance of me changing my mind. This already had been such a hard decision, to admit that I was a failure. I knew that if I couldn't even stick out one year, I probably wouldn't get another position. Having spent all that time and money renovating the home (the best home we ever had until that point), I realized I would have to leave all that behind and find a job somewhere else. Furthermore, I would have to uproot our children, who had really come to enjoy that place.

On Monday morning, my wife wanted to use the car, so she drove me to school. Before she dropped me off, I said to her, "I hope that God will confirm my decision somehow."

When she picked me up after school, she asked, "How was it?"

I said, "It wasn't any worse, but neither was it any better. I just dragged myself through the day."

She said, "That's interesting, I was praying and fasting, and God seemed to say that He was going to speak to us today."

Her comment was "music to my ears" because for the past one and a half months, the windows of Heaven seemed like brass. Although I was learning some things, overall, God was silent. Now He was going to speak!

"I am going to wait until after supper to hand in my written resignation," I told my wife.

I went directly into our bedroom and prayed. I don't remember a thing I prayed, but all of a sudden God spoke, not in an audible voice, but it was so clear in my spirit. He said, "Henry, if I have led you in, you're in until I lead you out. Going through hardship does not mean leading you out." Now, in the natural sense, this message should have been discouraging; it meant that I had to stay in this unbearable situation. But the only way I can describe this event was to say it was as if the whole room lit up and I was free! That heavy darkness that was over me was gone. I went to the telephone and called the superintendent and said, "I've changed my mind; I'm going to stay!" He said, "Good! I've discovered that those anonymous phone calls were all from the same lady, who is a trouble maker in the district. Nobody pays attention to her."

The parents hadn't turned against me as I had been led to believe! As soon as I hung up the telephone, it rang. It was the pastor's wife of the church we had attended before we moved. She said, "We would like to come and visit for a few days, would that be all right?" Delighted, I exclaimed, "Could you come?" Since the church had seemingly turned against me, I felt that nobody understood, and now I would be able to share with the pastor and his wife. For the first time since I had become injured, I could miraculously move without pain, and I knew the ribs were healed.

The next morning when I walked into the classroom, the students greeted me with a friendly, "Hi Mr. Warkentin!" They were right back to where they had been in September and October. I had not done anything to turn them against me, and I didn't do anything that made them turn back to me. I saw so clearly that God had given the devil permission to work through those students to bring me to the end of myself, and now had restricted the Enemy to do anything further. I'm sure the students never knew why they had been so disrespectful. They were used by the Enemy to act in an obnoxious way. The students still loved me, and for the rest of that year, I had their respect and cooperation, but now I was a changed person. I now entered a rest that I had never known before.

Before, if a person came for counseling from a long distance away, I would feel responsible to provide a solution. While they were yet talking, I was already trying to come up with answers for them. This was stressful and a heavy burden. Therefore, I was unable to fully listen to what they were saying. Now that I knew that without Christ I could do nothing, why even try? If God chooses to use me as a vessel, I can take no credit for what He does. However, if nothing happens, then I don't need to take any blame. I couldn't *make* it happen even if I tried. I can rest while God does the work. Now, I can counsel from eight in the morning till midnight, and not even be tired. I thank God for allowing the Enemy to bring me to the point of recognizing my total helplessness. His strength was truly made perfect in weakness.

I have found that it is better to pray, "God make me weak." When we are weak, *He* is our strength. I do not want to give the impression that I have arrived, for I have not yet learned to apply these truths in every area of my life; it is a process. But to whatever area that I have learned to apply these, it is true, *"For my yoke is easy, and my burden is light"* (Matthew 11:30).

Testing the Application

God wants us to apply these life-changing principles to different circumstances in our lives. For example, I used to enjoy teaching math. It was satisfying to teach my students a new concept and to show them systematically how to arrive at the solution. Eventually, the students said they understood the concept, and I could see by their eyes they understood. As a teacher, I knew that if I didn't give them many different problems to practice, they would not retain it. After they had done about twenty problems, applying the concept in different ways, we could leave it and go on to the next concept. God is the best teacher I know, and He also gives us different trials to help us learn how to establish the truth we're learning.

God wants His Word to bear fruit in us. Before a farmer sows the grain, he cultivates the land and sometimes he even plows it (turning it literally upside down) in order to receive the seed and bear much fruit. In order for the Word of God to bear fruit in our lives, God allows the Enemy to "cultivate" us, and sometimes turn us upside down, as it were.

Dry Spells

Sometimes we go through dry spells in our Christian walk, which we don't like. It seems that God takes away our awareness of His manifested presence in our lives. We usually see no value in such times and, therefore, find it hard to be patient.

One particular year, when I was still farming, I seeded the grain in the spring. The plants came up and the rains came, causing them to grow lush and green. Throughout that summer, the grain never suffered because the rains always came on time. The grain grew very tall and looked very promising. After the grain was fully-grown, the only thing left to happen was that the grain had to fill up the kernels. Suddenly, we hit a dry spell, and the kernels shriveled. Everything had looked so promising, and now, what a disappointment!

The following year, the exact opposite happened. As soon as the plants came up, there was a dry spell and the plants were yellowish and sickly. When a rain finally came, the plants revived and then another dry spell hit. The plants limped through the whole summer in this manner. It did not look nearly as promising as the year before. When the grain was fully grown and all it had to do was fill up the kernels, we hit one final dry spell. I thought that the crop this year too was also going to be a failure. To my utter surprise, the kernels filled up, resulting in a good crop.

As I pondered the difference between those two years, I understood what had happened. In the first year, because the rains always came, the moisture stayed at the top of the soil, so the roots grew horizontally. After the roots quit growing and the water table receded, the roots could not reach the water they needed and, therefore, the kernels shriveled. In the second year, however, the dry spells in the growing season caused the roots to grow deep in search of water. At the end of the season, although there was a dry spell again, the roots were drawing water from below.

In our Christian walk, we tend to believe that God is good if He always showers us with blessings. We prefer this, but it doesn't prepare us for the trials that are so essential in our lives. It is when we have nothing tangible to depend upon that we exercise our faith and trust in God. When God permits the devil to hinder our awareness of God in our life, God is teaching us to walk by faith, and not by sight or feelings.

We do not often realize how valuable hardships and trials are. For instance, my dad died when I was twelve years old. Our home was uninsulated and heated by a wood stove. I had to go and cut firewood probably twelve to fifteen cords per winter. We had tall poplars on our farm, and if I went out into the middle of the bush, I could cut down a large number of trees in one day. However, I hated to cut the trees at the edge of the bush. A tree of the same diameter on the edge of the bush took me three or four times as long to cut down as the ones in the middle. The trees along the edge had to weather the storms on their own, and so the fibres were strong and hard. The trees in the middle of the bush, however, were protected by each other and their fibres were soft and thus much easier to cut down. In contrast, the trees on the edge of the bush gave off far more heat than the trees in the middle of the bush. I knew that if I cut down all the trees in the middle of the bush and left one standing, the first good breeze would have broken it down because it simply had no strength of its own.

If God protected us from trials, we would be such fragile Christians. Therefore, I thank God for all the trials He has allowed the Enemy to bring my way so I could be strong in the Lord and in the power of His might. Therefore, when we complain about the trials, instead of embracing them, we miss out on God's best.

The Sifting of Peter: *Luke 22:31-62; John 21:1-22; Acts 2:38-41*

This fascinating account of the sifting of Peter begins on the day when Jesus went to Gethsemane after they celebrated the Passover. Jesus turns to (Simon) Peter and speaks the following warning:

> *And the Lord said, Simon, Simon, behold, Satan hath desired to have you, that he may sift you as wheat: but I have prayed for thee that thy faith fail not, and when thou art converted,* [returned] *strengthen thy brethren* (Luke 22:31-32).

Jesus gave the devil permission to sift Peter so that Peter would be able to strengthen the brethren at a future time. Until then, there had been a lot of "self" in Peter. He didn't recognize it, but Jesus saw it. Peter had to be refined in order to be useful. Satan desired to destroy Peter or to at least give him a very difficult time. As I pondered one day what it meant *"To sift you as wheat,"* I was reminded of a farming memory I have as a child:

When it came time to plant, my dad would choose the best wheat for seed. He would set this wheat aside and would have us children sift it. We didn't need to sift the rest of the wheat, but only the wheat that was going to be used for seed. My dad would pick a screen with just the right sized holes for wheat. In a similar way, God allows the devil to use only certain things to sift us.

Next, my dad would suspend one end of the screen from the ceiling with a rope; on the other end there were two handles, which were held in our hands. He would then pour some wheat on the screen, and we would shake the screen back and forth, making the wheat slide from end to end. The wheat would slide back and forth over the screen, bumping into the sides. That is how our lives often feel as well. We see no reason for the bumpy, unsteady ground beneath us.

Some of the wheat would fall through the screen. When we, too, are sifted, it can feel as if the "bottom falls out" of our world, and we struggle to hang on to something firm.

After all the wheat fell through, the residue remaining on the top of the screen was then dumped into the garbage, and the clean wheat was used for seed. I personally hated this job; it was boring, tedious, and dusty. Isn't it amazing that the devil gets to do the dirty job of sifting?

The wheat needed to be cleaned because, often, there would be dead grasshoppers, pieces of straw, or other unwanted trash scattered amongst the wheat. If one of these "foreign objects" remained among the seed, it would plug the seed drill. Then, instead of the seed being planted to bring forth fruit, the weeds would grow there because they would have no competition.

In a similar way, Jesus allowed the devil to sift out the impurities in Peter that would hinder him from bearing fruit in the Kingdom of God.

How Did the Devil Sift Peter?

Peter's response to the Lord was, *"Lord, I am ready to go with thee, both into prison and to death"* (Luke 22:33). The confidence in the flesh that Peter exhibited by this statement was just like the trash we had to remove from the seed.

Jesus responded, *"I tell thee Peter, the cock shall not crow this day, before that thou shalt thrice deny that thou knowest me"* (Luke 22:34). Jesus knew the imperfections in Peter and knew beforehand how Peter was going to respond in the flesh, accepting the fear that Satan would impose on him.

Jesus then turned to the rest of the disciples saying,

...When I sent you without purse, and scrip, [food bag] and shoes, lacked ye any thing? And they said, Nothing. Then said he unto them, but now he that hath a purse, let him take it and likewise his scrip: and he that hath no sword, let him sell his garment and buy one (Luke 22:35-36).

Why did Jesus make sure they would have a sword? He had also taught them that if somebody struck them on the left cheek, they were to turn to him the right cheek as well (Matthew 5:39). Now, Jesus was making sure that they would have a sword, even if they had to sell their garment: *"And they said unto him, Lord, behold, here are two swords, and he said unto them, it is enough"* (Luke 22:38).

By His statements, we can see that Jesus knew exactly what the devil would do through Peter if there were a sword available. When the High Priest's guards came to arrest Jesus, He walked up to the mob and asked who they were looking for. They said, *"Jesus of Nazareth."* He said, *"I am He,"* and they all fell down. By this incident, Peter should have seen Jesus didn't need any help from him. In fact, in Matthew 26:53, Jesus said, *"I could call for twelve legions of angels,"* but He didn't.

What was being sifted in Peter when he took that sword and chopped off the servant's ear? Peter looked at things from an *earthly perspective*, thinking, "My master is in danger; I've got to do something!" Instead, Jesus was showing His power to Peter by healing the ear of Peter's enemy, the wound that Peter himself had caused. Oh, what a crash-course Peter was going through!

Jesus was arrested, and they took Him to the High Priest's house, Peter following afar off. After those in the hall kindled the fire, Peter sat down among them. When the maids accused him of being Jesus' disciple, he denied it vehemently three times. Right then, the cock crowed. Jesus turned and looked at Peter from where He was. Peter remembered Jesus' prediction that, before the cock crowed, he would deny Him three times. The look Jesus had on His face when He met Peter's eyes was not of condemnation, nor did it say "I told you so;" rather, His face was full of compassion and understanding. This was the incident that obviously broke Peter, and he went out and wept bitterly.

Peter's confidence and his dependence on himself was shrinking. As Jesus was going to be put to death, Peter was unable to protect Him. Worse still, he had been a coward in denying even knowing Him.

The disciples, including Peter, had never understood that Jesus was going to die and rise again, although He had told them many times over. They still believed that Jesus was going to set up an earthly kingdom, and they were vying for a position within that kingdom. When Jesus was crucified, their hopes were shattered.

When He arose again on the third day, their hopes probably arose, too. They must have thought, "We did not understand Jesus' dying and rising, but now that He is raised from the dead, this time He is going to set up the kingdom." He had shown Himself to them three times after the resurrection and still made no move towards doing what they expected Jesus should do.

We often get discouraged when God does not do what we expect, and so we are tempted to go back to what is familiar. This is what Peter tried to do. But like Peter, if we try to go back, we are sure to fail in that thing, and never receive fulfillment through it:

> *Simon Peter saith to the rest of them, I go a fishing. They say unto him, We also go with thee. They went forth, and entered a ship immediately; and that night they caught nothing (John 21:3).*

In other words, Peter was saying, "I will go back fishing, forget about this faith stuff, and return to what is predictable." Some of the other disciples decided to go with him. Yet, as this Scripture indicates, the men couldn't even succeed in their old profession of fishing anymore. There were many fish in that sea. So, why didn't they catch any? After all, they were experienced fishermen who knew when to fish, where to fish, and how to fish. I believe that they didn't catch any fish, because demons in the water were hitting the fish on the noses when they headed to the net. The devil was still doing the sifting, and it was the devil that wanted all the disciples to be discouraged, to quit following Jesus, and, ultimately, to have them destroyed. Though all the disciples were being tested, the focus was definitely on Peter, and in essence, the rest of the disciples were affected by his sifting as well.

The disciples came back to shore after utter failure and there stood Jesus, ready to receive the discouraged failures. He knew what the devil had done because He had given him permission to do it.

> *Then Jesus saith unto them, Children, have ye any meat? and they answered him, No. And he said unto them, Cast the net on the right side of the ship and you shall find. They cast therefore, and now they were not able to draw it for the multitude of fishes* (John 21:5-6).

Every fisherman knows it doesn't matter what side of the boat the net hangs on! Jesus, in calling them "children," was saying something about their fragile faith.

Up till this point, Peter had evaluated everything through his natural, earthly understanding. This was apparent when he cut off the servant's ear. But Peter was now showing some progress. He and the disciples now obeyed Jesus, although what He said made no sense. Aren't many of us tempted to evaluate things according to our natural senses and understanding, instead of simply trusting and obeying God?

After the disciples returned to shore, a startling drama took place. (See John 21:15-23.) Jesus asked Peter, *"Simon son of Jonas, lovest thou me more than these?"* Peter exclaimed, *"... I love thee!"* Jesus asked him the same question two more times and Peter affirmed his answer each time: "Lord, you know I love you." Three times, he had denied Jesus, and now, three times he expresses his love for Him.

Jesus did this to Peter in order to reinstate him as a disciple. Peter had passionately denied being a disciple, and Jesus took him at his word. How do we know Peter was no longer a disciple? When the women met the man dressed in white at the empty tomb (Mark 16:7), He said, "Go tell my disciples *and Peter.*" By allowing the devil to sift Peter, enabling him to become a mature disciple, Jesus showed His great love for Peter. Jesus just wouldn't let Peter go!

But Jesus addressed Peter further, saying,

Verily, Verily I say unto thee, when thou wast young, thou girdest thyself, and walkest wither thou wouldst, but when thou shalt be old, thou shall stretch forth thy hands and another shall gird thee and carry thee wither thou wouldst not. This spake he signifying by what death he should glorify God. And when he had spoken this, he saith unto him, Follow me (John 21:18).

This statement would not seem to be very encouraging for Peter, and Peter, looking around and seeing John said to Jesus, *Lord what shall this man do?* (John 21:21), meaning, "If this is going to happen to me, what about John?" *And Jesus said unto him, If I will that he tarry till I come, what is that to thee? Follow thou me* (John 21:22).

Fifty days later, at the Feast of Pentecost, Peter preached the first message, and three thousand souls were saved. That marks an incredible transformation in the life of Peter. I am personally convinced that if Jesus had not allowed the devil to sift Peter, the three thousand souls would not have been saved because Peter likely would have preached from his own strength. When God allows the devil to harass us, He is not doing this out of punishment. Rather, He sifts us so that we can come to full stature and can be fully used by God, receiving the blessing of mature sonship.

"Jesus came that we may have life and have it more abundantly" (John 10:10). Unless the "self" is sifted out, we cannot receive abundant life. Peter's sifting was not just for his own benefit, but after he was sifted and his faith strengthened, he was to strengthen the brethren, not selfishly hoarding, but rather, feeding the sheep. Again, we see God's plan for the believer—refinement to become a useful vessel.

CHAPTER TEN

Depending on God

WHEN ADAM AND EVE chose to eat of the forbidden fruit, what they really chose was independence from God. If they had chosen to eat from the Tree of Life, it would have meant total dependence on God, and He would have directed them every step of their lives. He would have then been Lord of their lives. They chose instead to eat of the fruit from the Tree of Knowledge of Good and Evil because they wanted to make decisions for themselves and attain independence from God. This was the opposite of what God had intended for them. Everyday, we are faced with the same decision—either to eat of the Tree of Life or of the tree of Knowledge of Good and Evil. Everyday, the Enemy tries to influence our perspective through self-centredness, independence, and worldliness, whether we are aware of it or not.

Since that time, God has desired to reverse this independence in us. This independence caused fellowship to be broken, and His main concern is to make us Christ-like so that He can have fellowship with us again. Dependence upon Him is part of that fellowship, in the same way that Jesus was dependent on His Father:

> *Then answered Jesus and said unto them, Verily, verily, I say unto you, The Son can do nothing of himself, but what he seeth the Father do: for what things soever he doeth, these also doeth the Son likewise. For the Father loveth the Son, and showeth him all things that himself doeth: and he will show him greater works that these, that ye may marvel* (John 5:19-20).

When we are independent, we are not Christ-like. When children grow up and become adolescents, often there is a push to become independent of their parents, which is a natural thing. However, to become independent of God is not valuable. Since the Garden of Eden, it has been God's desire to reverse this independence

"Let Go—Jesus Will Catch You"

I once counseled a gentleman named George. He had his own road construction business. During the late 70's, when things were going well economically, he bought new machinery and incurred a debt of $600,000. The economy then reversed, the government cutting back on road building, leaving him without employment. The interest rates went up, and he was on the verge of bankruptcy. He recognized that God was teaching him many things through this, but he kept praying that God would finish the work in him before he went bankrupt.

My heart went out to George because I could see that he was resisting the very thing that God wanted to do in his life. His prayer to avoid bankruptcy was a natural reaction, but it exposed that he was unable to fully trust God with this. He could not come to the point of accepting that God was in control and that he could just rest in that fact. I shared with him that God sometimes arranges failure in our lives.

I could see that George wanted to believe this truth, but the humiliation of going through bankruptcy seemed too much. That same evening, while we were attending a service, the speaker had a word of knowledge for George, and he called him up to the front. He said, "I see you hanging onto a rope, and you are sliding down the rope. Now you have come to the end of the rope and there is a knot, and you are holding on with every bit of strength that you have." I thought the next thing he was going to say was, "Hang on, hang on, brother!" Instead, with great wisdom he said, "Let go—Jesus is standing there to catch you."

Death and Resurrection

Jesus said, *"Except a corn of wheat fall into the ground and die it abideth alone"* (John 12:24). A kernel of wheat holds life within it, but if it laid in a granary for ten years, nothing would happen to it. There is life in the kernel, but nothing will happen until the farmer puts that kernel of wheat into the ground. Then the temperature, moisture, and pressure will work on that kernel of wheat until the outer shell is broken and the life within it is released. This is a beautiful picture of the Christian life. When you are born-again, you have spiritual life within you, but unless the outer shell, the "self-life," gets broken, that new spiritual life will be boxed in, and for all purposes, will be useless, as far as the Christian walk is concerned.

I thought I had a talent in teaching, but when God arranged failure, my talent meant nothing. In fact, every talent that God gives us has to go through a death experience and a resurrection. Without death and resurrection, there is no spiritual life, for even Jesus had to die and be raised again.

We sometimes look at a gifted person and are tempted to say, "If he only became a Christian, what great things he could do for God!" But where did those talents come from? The Bible clearly says *"whatever is born of the flesh is flesh"* (John 3:6). Just because we become Christians does not make our talents "Christian." We can focus our talents on good things, but unless they have gone through a death and resurrection process, they will not produce gold, silver, and precious stones, but only wood, hay, and stubble.

Jesus spoke about a sower sowing seeds. Some of the seed fell by the wayside, and the birds came and took it away (Matthew 13:3). Most of us have received a large portion of seed, but much of it does not bear fruit because the soil is not prepared. I have never seen a farmer throwing the seeds on hard soil. He first tills the ground and sometimes even plows it, literally turning the soil upside down.

God is the best Teacher and Master farmer when it comes to our spiritual lives. He will plow us, but not for the sake of destroying or hurting us. He prepares our soil for His seed, that we will bear much fruit. Maybe you feel plowed right now—remember, God is a God of love, and the kindest thing He can do is plow us. His purposes are not limited to this world but are invested for eternity.

God will take us through death-like experiences. For example, this happened to me when my teaching was stripped; God also took my counseling through shipwreck.

About a year after this "stripping," I was asked to be the director of the Christian Enrichment Family Camp. I prayed, "God, why didn't you ask me two years ago when I had all kinds of things to offer? I have nothing to offer now." The answer came back, "Why do you think I chose the common fisherman to be my disciples?" I said, "All right, God, I get the message. You do not need my qualifications nor talents; all You want of me is to be a willing vessel. I choose to be willing to take the position as director, provided You keep the responsibility for the camp."

During that first summer at camp, there were many opportunities to rest in the knowledge that God was carrying the responsibility for what would happen. One time, a half-hour before a meeting was to start, I did not know who the song leader or the speaker would be. The speaker, too, was supposed to arrive early, but he had not shown up yet, so we were without a song leader *and* a speaker.

I remember standing outside talking to a friend about not having found a speaker or song leader. I remember myself saying, "I'm glad that it is not my problem—it's God's." As we were talking, my friend asked me if I had asked a certain man who was walking by us to lead the singing. "No, I don't even know him." I went running after him and asked, "Have you ever led praise and worship before?" He affirmed that he had and that he was very willing to do it that evening. The song leader had been found, but I still had no speaker.

That evening, the gentleman led the worship and after-wards, I opened the service for testimonies. People's lives were deeply touched as two people gave moving life-changing testimonies. The people were as impacted by these testimonies as they probably would have been by a powerful message.

A question that is often raised is, "What good are the talents we have prior to their death and resurrection?" Talents are just for this temporary world, but if they go through death and resurrection, they will produce eternal results. Death comes when you can lay the talent aside and say, "God, it is all right if you never use this talent in me again," and you are able to recognize that without Him, you can do nothing. The

Bible is the Word of God, but it is dead doctrine unless God resurrects it in you, causing it to come alive.

Aaron's Rod

In Numbers 16-17, the children of Israel grumble and challenge Aaron that God speaks only through him, and not through them. To settle the matter, God commands all those who are the "Head" of their family to place their rods (the primary symbol of authority) in the Tabernacle along with Aaron's rod:

And it shall come to pass, that the man's rod, whom I shall choose, shall blossom: and I will make to cease from me the murmurings of the children of Israel, whereby they murmur against you (Numbers 17:5).

All night, the rods laid there. But in the morning,

... Moses went into the tabernacle of witness; and behold, the rod of Aaron for the house of Levi was budded, and brought forth buds, and bloomed blossoms, and yielded almonds (Numbers 17:8).

All of those rods had been alive at one time because they were wood, but now they were all dead wood. In the morning, they saw that Aaron's rod had budded; it had come to life—it had resurrection life.

It was required that those rods be relinquished. They were placed before God for an entire night, out of the reach of their owners.

I don't know how long your "night experience" will be, but in the end, I am confident that in the areas of your life that you relinquish, there will be resurrection life.

In this incident with Aaron and the Israelites, God was saying, "I have given resurrection life to Aaron, and I will use his ministry." This is the principle by which God operates, and when we begin to see this, we will not want to hold onto our talents or abilities. We will let go of the rod, as it were, and let God decide how and what He wants to use.

When my counseling and teaching had gone through shipwreck, I was embarrassed to think that Christians would find out that I had degrees in secular theories, when in the end I found out that the problems were spiritual and these theories provided no answers. The Lord quickened to me what Paul said when he talked about all his training and credentials, that he counted it all as dung. Paul spoke of his accomplishments not with regret and shame, but with the humble knowledge that apart from God, those attainments were worthless.

Finally, I realized that God was showing me that the credentials I could have relied upon and the results in the natural would have been worthless.

Gradually, though, some of my training became useful. God was resurrecting it. Today, I do not know what percentage of this secular education I use. But I do know that when God strips us, He brings us to the point where we know that we know that we *know* that without Him we can do nothing. Talents work only as long as He sustains them. After they have gone through a death process, you will know that you have to depend on Him alone:

> *I am crucified with Christ: nevertheless I live; yet not I, but Christ liveth in me: and the life which I now live in the flesh I live by the faith of the Son of God, who loved me and gave himself for me* (Galatians 2:20).

When we grasp this truth, we can start resting. This is the measure of success in the eyes of God—dependence on Him.

Death and resurrection is the procedure for eternity. We may have done great things and may have ministered to people in our own strength, but that does not produce gold and silver.

The Sun Went Down

And he [Jacob] *lighted upon a certain place, and tarried there all night, **because the sun was set**; and he took of the stones of that place, and put them for his pillows, and lay down in the place to sleep* [emphasis mine] (Genesis 28:11).

When Jacob ran away from Esau and stayed at Bethel, the sun went down. Why would it be important to mention that the sun went down?

And Jacob asked him, and said, Tell me, I pray thee, thy name. And he said, Wherefore is it that thou dost ask after my name? And he blessed him there. And Jacob called the name of the place Peniel: for I have seen God face to face, and my life is preserved. And as he passed over Peniel the sun rose upon him, and he halted upon his thigh (Genesis 32:29).

After Jacob wrestled with God and was blessed, the sun rose. There was a sunset and a sunrise. Similarly, when Aaron and the other priests put their rods down, they went through the night, and by morning, Aaron's rod had budded. Jacob, too, wrestled all night, and in the morning, he had a breakthrough.

God injured Jacob in the thigh. The thigh is the strongest part of our body. Relating this to our own lives, we may find we give God control of the weaker areas, but we usually hang onto the areas where we feel we are strong.

When God touched Jacob's hip and made him lame, it was a reminder to him for the rest of his life, that his own strength was rendered useless.

We, like Jacob, have night seasons; Jacob's lasted over twenty years. We do not know how long our night is going to be, but we can be confident that the morning will come. The Bible tells us that for everything there is a season (Ecclesiastes 3:1), and we can be encouraged that when it ends, the next one will begin.

Valleys and Mountaintops

Often these "night" times in our lives are likened to valleys. It is in valleys where we find green food. It is in the valley that we are fed spiritually. If you were a shepherd and had many sheep to tend, where would you take them—to a mountaintop or to a valley? You would take them to the valley because that is where you could feed them.

Jesus is the Good Shepherd. Don't you think He is going to take us to the valley? Later, when we are able to stand on the mountaintop, we can see what we have come through and all we have eaten. It is on the mountaintop where we can praise God for the valley and for what He has done in our lives. You cannot go very far on the mountaintop before you have to go downhill again. However, it is far easier going down from that position than it is going up. It is God's desire to help us develop a contentment for the valleys.

Vision and Death

God can give you a vision, but this vision will also have to go through a death process. God gave Joseph the vision that he was going to be a ruler, but how much of that looked real to him when he was sold as a slave? When he later became the top man at Potiphar's house, he must have thought that this was the beginning of the fulfillment of the vision given to him. But he was then thrown into jail for standing up for the truth of God's principles, landing right back at the bottom, only to rise again later as ruler. I am encouraged by the story of Joseph because he could have easily become bitter. Instead, he became better. God strips us and prepares us so that future success will not be our ruin.

A successful minister asked God once, "Why do You take all the glory for Yourself? Why don't You share it with Your children?" God answered him: "I am the only one who can take it and not be destroyed by it." Joseph went through all these preparations and finally he was ready to be used by God in a great way without it destroying him.

It was said of King Saul that when he was small in his own eyes, then he did great things. This was because God was doing great things through him. However, when Saul became important in his own eyes, he lost everything—the kingdom, his sanity, respect, and, eventually, his life.

If you desire to go all the way with God, you do not have to worry how He will work this "death" in your life, for it is His job, and He will do it. However, He needs your willingness to have it done. This is dependence on Him.

CHAPTER ELEVEN

The Exchanged Life

A S CHRISTIANS, WE ARE aware our lives need to be
changed, so we focus on affecting this change, and thus
focus on self rather than on Christ. This sets us up for defeat
and discouragement. We do not need a "changed life," but
even more, we need the "exchanged life." We need revelation
to understand that only Christ's Life in us can produce this
change in us (Galatians 2:20).[4]

The Difference of One Letter

Now to Abraham and his seed were the promises made.
He saith not, And to seeds, as of many; but as of one,
And to thy seed, which is Christ (Galatians 3:16).

Paul saw by revelation the significance of one single
letter—the letter "s". What is the significance of Paul referring to Abraham's "seed" (singular) rather than "seeds"
(plural)? If it had been "seeds," then the promise made to
Abraham would have referred to his direct descendants—

Israel. However, it says the *seed*—referring to Christ—which includes all believers. Verse 29 concludes, *"And if ye be Christ's, then are ye Abraham's seed, and heirs according to the promise."* The promises that are given to Abraham and his seed are also given to us. What a revelation that one letter makes.

In the first five chapters of Romans, Paul talks about "sins," and then starting in chapter six, he talks about "sin." Again, we have a significant truth tied up in the use of one letter. The significance is that "sins" are the actions, the overt things that we commit. The blood of Jesus dealt with those sins. Hebrews 9:22b tells us *"...and without the shedding of blood is no remission* [of sins]. *"* We have committed sins, and we need forgiveness and cleansing through the blood of Christ. However, that does not deal with "sin." "Sin" refers to the *sinner*, the factory that produces the "sins." God had to make a different provision to deal with "sin." The Cross is the tool He chose to deal with it.

The blood deals with our "sins," but our position in Adam allows the factory to remain. If we have received everything that was in Adam, then somehow we must get out of Adam. But How? The blood of Jesus Christ does not take us out of Adam. Death is the secret of emancipation:

> *What shall we say then? Shall we continue in sin that grace may abound? God forbid. How shall we that are dead to sin, live any longer therein? Know ye not, that so many of us as were baptized in Jesus Christ were baptized into his death?* (Romans 6:1-3).

If God dealt with us in the position of Christ, how did we get into Christ? In Hebrews, the writer uses an interesting analogy of Abraham paying his tithes to Melchizedec:

176

The book says that Levi, who was *"in the loins"* of Abraham, paid the tithes to Melchizedec (Hebrew 7:10), but Abraham's descendants, Isaac and Jacob, weren't even born yet. Therefore, if Levi, the great-grandson of Abraham, who was in the loins of Abraham before he was born, paid tithes to Melchizedec, so you, in a similar way were in Adam. If my wife and I had been killed forty years ago, all my four children would have died in my loins. By the same principle, we were in Adam and received his nature. When he sinned, we sinned. However, by the same law, we are now in Christ and have His nature: *"But of him are ye in Christ Jesus, who of God is made unto us wisdom, and righteousness, and sanctification, and redemption"* (1 Corinthians 1:30). It is because of God that we are in Christ Jesus; God placed us in Christ Jesus. We were in Christ when He was crucified and, therefore, we were crucified.

Jesus did it alone. He died as our representative. Paul says in 1 Corinthians 15:45,47,

And so it is written, The first man Adam was made a living soul; the last Adam was made a quickening spirit... the first man was of the dust of the earth, the second man from heaven.

Notice it does not say the first Adam and the second Adam; it says the first Adam and the *last* Adam. Through the first man Adam, we received all that was in him. When Jesus came as the last Adam, everything that was in Adam was nailed to the cross. Jesus was the last, and there can be nothing beyond that which is last. The Enemy will always try to get us to focus on what we have to try to do to get out of Adam, thereby getting us to focus on "self." Nevertheless, the first Adam is finished because the last Adam, Jesus

Christ, finished everything that we ever inherited through Adam.

Jesus ended all that was started with Adam, thereby starting a new race. The first man started a sinful race; the second man started the *redeemed* race.

An Established Historical Fact

In order to have victory, we must realize that death—our death—is a historical fact. We are not dying to sin today; we are, in fact, dead to sin:

> *Knowing this, that our old man is crucified with him, that the body of sin might be destroyed, that henceforth we should not serve sin. For he that is dead is freed from sin. Now if we be dead with Christ, we believe we shall also live with him: Knowing that Christ being raised from the dead dieth no more; death hath no more dominion over him. For in that he died, he died unto sin once; but in that he liveth, he liveth unto God. Likewise reckon ye also yourselves dead indeed unto sin, but alive unto God through Jesus Christ our Lord.... Being then made free from sin, ye became the servants of righteousness* (Romans 6:6-11,18).

One of the reasons so many Christians walk around defeated is that they do not realize that the old Adamic nature is dead, and thus we are still trying to die to sin. Our old nature was alive to sin, but our new divine nature is not. This can be best reflected in Eve, who initially did not have a sin-nature, but had a self-nature. It was to this self-nature the serpent appealed. Often, Christians confuse the sin-nature with the self-nature and will continue trying to kill the sin-nature, which in Christ is already dead. For example, if you and I

178

were sitting in the same room and I commanded you, "Get *into* this room," you'd be puzzled because you know you're already in. No matter how hard you tried, whether you climbed the walls or laid on the floor, you would not get into the room anymore than you are now. It is the same with our position in Christ and our death to sin. We *are* dead, and no matter how hard we try, we can't "get in" any more than we already are.

It is an established historical fact. To obtain justification, we must see Christ bearing our sin on the cross. To obtain sanctification, we must see Christ bearing us on the cross.

How do we receive forgiveness? Do we ask Jesus to die again? No, we accept that He has already done it; it *is* a fact. In the same way, our deliverance is also a historical fact:

> *Knowing this, that our old man is crucified with him, that the body of sin might be destroyed, that hence-forth we should not serve sin. For he that is dead is freed from sin. Now if we be dead with Christ, we believe we shall also live with him* (Romans 6:6-8).

If we believe that Christ died for us, the same Scripture tells us that we, too, died. When did we die? When Christ died.

Can Christ's crucifixion be past and mine still be future? From the way we function, it often seems that way. On what grounds do we believe that Christ did die? Do we depend upon our feeling? Do we merely "feel" that Christ died? No! We do not "feel" that the world is round, yet we believe it is because we know it is a fact.

Our crucifixion was more intimate than the crucifixion of the thieves on the cross. They were crucified beside Jesus, but we were in Him when He died. If we feel that Christ died—He died. And if we do not feel that Christ died—He still died;

His death has nothing to do with our feelings. Whether the former self in us feels dead or not, it is, in fact, still dead. That Christ died is a fact, that the thieves died is a fact, and that we died is also—a fact.

The old sinful self that we hate is dead. Often we want to crucify our old self, but it is not possible. We cannot nail ourselves to a cross.

God's way of deliverance is different from ours. We try to suppress sin by seeking to overcome it, trying to become a stronger Christian.

Ye lust, and have not: ye kill, and desire to have, and cannot obtain: ye fight and war, yet ye have not because ye ask not. Ye ask, and receive not, because ye ask amiss, they ye may consume it upon your lusts (James 4:2-3).

Most Christians ask amiss for strength and power to overcome sin or trials by themselves. God wants us to become weaker. In 2 Corinthians 12:10, Paul says, *"...for when I am weak then I am strong."* Our prayer should be, "Oh God, make me so that I give up trying; rather, help me to depend upon what you have done." My daughter Carol's testimony, which she gave in church recently, illustrates this quite clearly:

I was a wonderful person—a good little Christian girl, you could have called me. While my friends were rebelling, angry with their parents and other authority figures, I did not—I was not even tempted to. Then I got married to Kevin... but still I was a wonderful person. Marriage was a fairly easy adjustment; in fact, our first fight was over the question of whether or not we had ever had a fight. I would hear people talk about their struggles with anger, and I would be relieved that I didn't have that problem. Then... I became a mother. Little did I realize when we brought that first little bundle of joy home from the hospital that I was about to be tested in ways I had never imagined. Within a very short period of time, sleepless nights, coupled with a crying baby whom I did not always know how to console, quickly brought me to the end of my patience. For the first time, I began to understand child abuse a little better! Feeling frustrated and helpless, anger would surge up within me, and the urge to pat his back a little bit harder, or to be a little bit more rough with him would be overwhelming. After the anger was gone, I would feel guilty and discouraged. As much as I would try to excuse my anger by focusing on my lack of sleep or some other such excuse, I was scared by the realization that I had within me the potential to hurt this innocent little child. I cried out to God for strength to help me not to get angry, but I would still have times of "losing it." As time went on, and we had more children, I learned better how to cope with my anger. When I would feel myself getting angry and sense that I was about to lose control, I would make myself leave the room, take some deep breaths, and wait until I was calmed down again before re-entering the situation. But still, I would sometimes "lose it," and my heart ached over what kind of example I was setting for my children. In the Bible, in 2 Corinthians, chapter 12, verses 9 & 10, Paul talks about God's strength being perfected in his weaknesses. Well, I knew that I was weak, but why was I not experienc-

ing God's strength? I prayed and prayed that God would make that truth become reality in my life.

*And then, just a short while ago, Kevin said something that stopped me dead in my tracks. He commented on the fact that I was carrying the burden of trying to raise perfect children. My eyes filled up with tears as the realization flooded over me, that I had not really been trusting God! While I had been crying out to God for help, I was still trusting in myself. With a broken heart, I repented before the Lord. I asked Him to forgive me for the sin of not trusting Him to take care of my children, and I let them go into His hands. I told God that I was choosing to trust Him to raise my children, and rather than asking God to strengthen me, I would rest in **His** strength. Over and over again the Bible says that God IS our strength—when we have God, we have His strength. I also asked that God would give me the grace, at the moment in which that anger would rear its ugly head, to choose to reject the anger and to rest in Him instead. A couple of days later, in dealing with one of our children, that all too familiar feeling of anger surged up within me. But almost at that same instant, I found myself saying "I love him, I love him" over and over again in my mind. And as I did so, the anger disappeared. Again, a few days later as our two youngest were both crying and crying at the same time, the feeling of anger rose up within, and this time, I found myself immediately thanking God for being my peace and thanking Him for the precious gift of our children. Once again, the anger vanished. Each time this occurs, I have the choice to accept the feeling of anger and act upon it,* *or I can choose to reject it and instead rest in God's strength. I know that this is a growing process which all began when I chose to "let go and let God," when I repented of trying to control each situation and chose to trust God instead. The peace and stress-free rest that I have been experiencing is absolutely incredible! What about you? Do you struggle with anger? If so, I want to encourage you to embrace this exciting truth:*

> *... "[Christ's] grace is sufficient for you, for [your] power is made perfect in weakness." Therefore [we can] boast all the more gladly about [our] weaknesses, so that Christ's power may rest on [us]* (2 Corinthians 12:9).

How do we know that our sins are forgiven? By revelation based on His Word. His Spirit bears witness with our spirit that we are children of God. How are we delivered from sin? The same way—through revelation, which is a divine fact. It has already happened; we are dead to sin!

Each person's experience will differ, but the revelation will be the same. I am praying that God will make that truth real to us because otherwise we will keep struggling and struggling to be dead to sin.

Abiding in Christ

In John 15:4, Jesus said,

> *Abide in me, and I in you. As the branch cannot bear fruit of itself, except it abide in the vine; no more can ye except ye abide in me.*

This verse means we are already in Him, and we do not need to struggle to get in. Jesus says, *"Abide in Me,"*—stay in that position, knowing that He has accomplished everything for us. Then we can walk in victory. We know that we cannot get into something when we are already in it.

One day, I heard a man give his testimony. He said, "Say I came to your house and asked you for a cup of coffee. While you were pouring the water into the kettle, I asked you again to please make me a cup of coffee. You assured me that you were in the process of doing that, and then again, I asked you for a cup of coffee. Your agitated reply would be, 'Can't you see that I am doing it?'" This is exactly what we do to God when we continue to ask for things that He has already given us.

Dead to Sin

We are already set free and dead to sin. What is a characteristic of death? There is no response to any stimuli.

A preacher related how he had many problems with his temper. He had grown up on the farm, and there they had a white cow that would often get through the fence into the grain field. Every morning when he got up, there was that cow in the grain! He would become angry and chase the cow out, trying to hurt it as much as he could.

He then came to the realization that he was sinning by giving into his anger. He determined that the next day he would *not* get angry—he was going to die to that sin of anger. The next morning, the cow was out again, and sure enough, he became angry.

One day, the truth that he was already dead to sin finally dawned on him. This time when he found the cow in the grain, he chased it out, singing praises to God. He was not responding any longer to the cause of his anger or trying to die to that anger.

Often, "we put the cart before the horse." If we count our-selves to be dead when we do not *know* we are dead, we will still lose our temper. Then the devil will say to us, "It doesn't work; you really aren't dead."

All of us can remember when we first realized that Christ died for us. It is equally important to know that we died *with* Christ. It is not that I count myself to be dead and, therefore, I am dead. Rather, I *am* dead and, therefore, count myself to *be* dead. Similarly, I do not reckon on being dead to sin, and then hope that I will be dead to it. I can say I am dead to sin because it is a fact—God's Word says so. We need to confess these truths because the devil will try to get us to believe otherwise.

God commands us to confess that we have died and then to abide by it. Romans 6:11 says, *"Likewise reckon ye also yourselves to be dead indeed unto sin, but alive unto God through Jesus Christ our Lord."*

Romans 6:3,6,9 encourages us to "know" what is truth. Then after we *know*, we can *reckon* what we know is true (as verse 11 tells us). The minister who was struggling with anger, first tried to reckon that he was dead before he *knew* the truth about being dead—thus, he remained defeated. After he received revelation truth that his death to sin was a fact, his temper had no power over him.

What happens when we recognize that some of those old desires rise up again, or we fall into known sin again? The devil will want us to doubt the divine fact that we are dead to sin. When you are faced with the temptation to give into doubt, this is an opportunity to make a decision: Are you going to believe what you see going around you, or are you going to believe the truth of God? Spiritual facts remain even though it may seem like the opposite is true. We have to believe that what God says is true, even though our senses tell us different.

Whosoever is born of God doth not commit sin; for his seed remaineth in him: he cannot sin, because he is born of God (1 John 3:9).

Have you ever found this verse difficult to comprehend? If we are born of God, then Christ lives in us and it is not in the nature of our new life in Christ for us to sin. In fact, the new life in us cannot sin; it is not in our nature to sin. The fact of a thing, and the history of the thing, are two different phenomena.

The Natural Law and Precedence

The nature of wood is to float. Now, suppose a piece of wood is pulled under water 90 percent of the time. It would be incorrect to think that the wood can no longer float just because it is under water. In a similar way, the nature of the new life in us is not to sin, but there may be times when the Enemy attacks and we are off guard, and he pulls and pushes us down.

Our experience is that we did indeed sin, but it doesn't change the fact that the nature of our new life is not to sin. Unless we recognize this truth and receive it, the devil will get us to doubt and look to ourselves again. Then we are back in the process of *trying* to become dead to sin.

Adam and Eve were created with a neutral nature. This nature was neither sinful nor divine. If they would have partaken of the fruit of the Tree of Life, choosing to be totally God-centred, they would have received a divine nature. However, since they chose the fruit of the Tree of Knowledge of Good and Evil, thus choosing self-centredness, they received a sinful nature. Therefore, through the first Adam's sin, we were born sinners and received a sinful nature. However, through Christ, who was the last Adam (1 Corinthians 15:45), our sin-nature, or our "old man" is crucified. As Paul puts it in Romans 6:6,

Knowing this, that our old man is crucified with him, that the body of sin might be destroyed, that hence-forth we should not serve sin.

So the old sin-nature is dead and buried. Through Christ's resurrection, we are raised to newness of life (Romans 6:4,5). Therefore, we now have a divine nature. Paul says in 1 Corinthians 15:49, *"And as we have borne the image of the earthy, we shall also bear the image of the heavenly."*

Since Eve did not have a sin-nature before the fall, the urge to sin did not originate from within but was imposed by the devil from without. Likewise, since every Christian now has a divine nature and Christ lives in him, the urge to sin also does not come from within but is imposed by the devil. John says in 1 John 3:9,

Whosoever is born of God doth not commit sin; for his seed [Jesus] remaineth in him: and he cannot sin, because he is born of God.

Even though Eve did not have a sin-nature, the devil appealed to her flesh and was able to deceive her into believing it was her desire to be self-centred and independent, and she acted upon it. In a similar way, even though the Christian now has a divine nature instead of a sin-nature, the devil can still appeal to the flesh (the natural man) and persuade or beguile him to act upon imposed thoughts and feelings. The devil then seizes the opportunity to tempt the Christian to believe this action still originated from his sin-nature. If he accepts this lie, he is defeated, but if he stands on the truth that the old sin-nature is dead and, therefore, does not produce sin anymore, he is victorious.

Christians need to focus on the fact that they now have a divine nature and Christ desires to live His life through it to produce the fruit of the spirit. If we fail in an area, the failure was not produced by our divine nature, but we were deceived by the Enemy. God always looks at our hearts' motives and attitudes.

Some years ago, I was meditating on the words of Jesus in Matthew 5:48: *"Be ye therefore perfect, even as your Father which is in heaven is perfect."* It seemed to me that this was impossible for any Christian to obey. Then it struck me that it says, *"Be* perfect," not *"Become* perfect." If He had said "Become perfect," He would have referred to our actions or performance.

When a carpenter first starts in the trade, his workmanship will be far from perfect, but as he practices, his workmanship will become more and more perfect. Jesus, however, commands that every Christian, including a new Christian, is to be perfect *now*. This clearly indicates Jesus is not talking about performance or actions but about motives and attitudes. Every Christian can choose right now to have right and godly motives and attitudes, even though his actions will not always be perfect.

The Bible notes many individuals who had a perfect heart: Noah, Asa, David, etc. In 1 Chronicles 29:9, it says, *"... because with perfect heart they offered willingly to the Lord: and David the king also rejoiced with great joy."* None of these men were faultless, yet they had perfect hearts according to God's Word.

I really began to understand the words of Jesus when God brought to my remembrance an incident that happened when I was four and a half years old. Our family lived on a small farm in Manitoba, Canada. In the winter, my father had the cows and horses tied in the barn, which was on one side of the yard, while the round haystacks were on the other side. My dad would take a pitchfork and carry to the barn as much loose hay as he could lift to feed the animals.

On one particular day, my dad was gone for the day, and I was playing outside in the snow. I walked over to the stacks of feed and noticed the bottom half of a sweet clover stack was low enough for me to crawl up on. I discovered that I could take a thin layer of sweet clover and roll it up like a blanket. I then had what I thought was a bright idea. I would roll this roll of sweet clover across the yard to the barn so that my dad wouldn't need to carry it when he came home. All he would have to do is to fork it into the cows' and horses' mangers. I worked long and hard to get the big roll to the barn. When I finally got it to the barn, I felt so proud and could hardly wait until my dad came home. However, when he came home and saw what I had done, he scolded me. What my little mind had not understood was that when I rolled the sweet clover across the yard, all the dry, brittle leaves broke off. I had brought only the thick stems of the sweet clover to the barn, and all the food value for the animals was lost! Had my dad looked at my heart, however, he would have seen that my heart was perfect towards him. My motive and attitude was to save him working time. If my dad would have looked at my heart, he would have praised me for what I did for him, but then would have used this incident to teach me that it was not good for the cows: *"... for man looketh on the outward appearance, but the Lord looketh on the heart"* (1 Samuel 16:7b).

In Romans 7, Paul treats sin as if it were a live person or being, not just a force or concept:

I had not known sin, but by the law: for I had not known lust except the law had said, Thou shalt not *covet. But **sin taking occasion** by the command-ment, **wrought in me** all manner of concupis-cence.... For sin, taking occasion by the command-ment, **deceived me**, and **by it slew me**.... Now if I do that I would not, it is no more I that do it, but sin that dwelleth in me. I find then a law, that when I would do good, evil is present with me. For I delight in the law of God after the inward man: But I see another law in my members, warring against the law of my mind, and bringing me into **captivity to the law of sin** which is in my members* [emphasis mine] (Romans 7:7b-8,11,20-23).

The emphasized words indicate that Paul treats sin as a person or being. What is the difference between sin and the law of sin, as mentioned in verse 23? In physics, when an experiment is done repeatedly, and the same result is achieved time after time, it is considered a law. For example, if I hold my pen up and let go of it, it will fall to the ground. This is the law of gravity in action.

If I, as a man, choose to lust after a woman, that is sin, but I can also choose not to lust. However, if every time I see women and lust after them, namely, the action of lust is auto-matic and involuntary, then it is the law of sin. It is always a particular lustful demon that imposes that lust.

The Enemy wants us to believe that this is our old nature, so that we will try again to overcome it, thereby defeating us. If the Enemy can get us to try to kill the old nature, then we have lost sight of the truth. If I believe that I am fighting against the old nature again, I will be unable to reconcile the description in the Bible of a Christian. Therefore, I can't walk in that truth, joy, and peace of how God sees me.

Two Husbands?

> *Know ye not brethren, (for I speak to them that know the law,) how that the law hath dominion over a man as long as he liveth? For the woman which hath a husband is bound by the law to her husband as long as he liveth; but if the husband be dead, she is loosed from the law of her husband. So, then if, while her husband liveth, she be married to another man, she shall be called an adulteress: but if her husband be dead, she is free from the law; so that she is no adulteress, though she be married to another man* (Romans 7:1-4).

This passage speaks about being freed from the law, and unless we understand this truth, we will continue to try to *do* things for God. However, there is nothing we can ever do for God that would please Him: *"All our righteousness is as filthy rags"* (Isaiah. 64:6).

In order to be set free from the law of trying to please God, Paul, in Romans 7:1-6 uses the illustration of the two husbands and a wife.

This woman is married to a good man, but he makes high demands on her. There is nothing wrong with his demands, but she finds it impossible to meet them. There is another man whose demands are just as great, but he is loving and kind and would fulfill the demands for her. If only she could be married to this kind man! Unless her husband died, however, it would be an adulterous relationship. Her husband shows no signs of dying; in fact, it appears that he will outlive her. The only way she could be set free is to die herself, because the moment she dies, she would be free from her marriage bond.

The first husband represents the law, which makes righteous demands of us. However, we can never live up to them: *"For whosoever shall keep the whole law, and yet offend in one point, he is guilty of all"* (James 2:10). If we fail in any one thing, then we have failed altogether. The woman represents you and I, who were bound to the law, as she was to her husband. The husband had a right to make demands on her, and the law has a right to make demands on us. However, if she died, then her husband could no longer make demands on her. Likewise, since we died in Christ, the law cannot make demands on us anymore. Jesus represents the second husband, and He has fulfilled the law for us. Therefore, it is through death that we are freed from the law.

The Law of the Spirit of Life

Paul says in Romans 8:2, *"The law of the Spirit of life in Christ Jesus hath made me free from the law of sin and death."*

It is not only important to recognize that I am free from sin, but I am free from the *law* of sin. How am I to be delivered from the law of sin? If I hold my pen in the air and then let go of it, the law of gravity will operate. However, if I hold my pen out and don't release it, it will not obey the law of gravity because the law of life overrides the law of gravity. It is a higher law. We haven't done away with the law of gravity, but the law of life supercedes it, and the pen does not fall. The law of aerodynamics also supercedes or overrides the law of gravity, allowing birds and planes to fly; however, it does not do away with the law of gravity, it is simply a higher law.

The law of life, as noted in Romans 8:2, supercedes the law of sin. A small seed can fall into a crack between pieces of cement and, eventually, as that seed grows, it will break the cement. The law of life is so powerful, even in the natural,

192

that a tiny seed which is living will grow and break cement. Here we have the law of life in overriding action, but as long as we haven't recognized the law of life operating in our own lives, we will always try with self-effort to do what only the law of life can do.

How Is the Law of Life Manifested in Us?

I am crucified with Christ: nevertheless I live; yet not I, but Christ liveth in me: and the life which I now live in the flesh I live by the faith of the Son of God who loved me, and gave himself for me (Galatians 2:20).

Our choices determine our application of this truth. In Romans 7:19-20, Paul confesses his frustration,

For the good that I would I do not: but the evil which I would not, that I do. Now if I do that I would not, it is no more I that do it, but sin that dwelleth in me.

Paul uses the word "I" at least twenty times in verses 14-25. This is "I" without the Spirit, struggling to please God.

We need a new revelation of the law of the spirit of life that dwells in us:

But if the same Spirit of him that raised Jesus from the dead dwelleth in you, he that raised up Christ from the dead shall also quicken your mortal bodies by his Spirit that dwelleth in you (Romans 8:11).

There is no mountain ahead of us that is too big for the Spirit of life that is in us.

The moment we want to implement something in the spiritual with our willpower, we will hinder it, but if we let ourselves live in the new law, the old law can no longer govern us. As I illustrated with my pen, the law of gravity is still there, but it does not hinder as long as the law of life is governing it. Birds are not afraid of the law of gravity. Although *we* know they are too heavy to fly, they don't know that, and so, they fly. We know, however, that the law of gravity is still working on them because every now and then we will see a dead bird on the ground—the law of gravity has taken over because death causes the law of life to cease.

We will often struggle if Christ has not been revealed in us *as our life*. We then keep running to God to help us in the area of need. For example, when a child first makes sounds and the mother understands that a certain sound means that the child wants milk, she will give the child milk. After a while, although the child makes that same sound, the mother will not give the child the milk, but waits until the child says "milk" properly. Later, after the child can say "milk" properly, she quits again and waits until the child is able to say, "Please give me milk." This is not harsh. This is proper child-training.

When a person is first born-again, he may tend to believe that he is spiritual. Soon he discovers that he loses his temper or fails in some area, at which point he runs to God and asks for more patience or some other quality. God recognizes that he is a babe and gives him patience, but the patience doesn't last. So the believer is required to run back for more patience. He is still seeing God outside of himself, as one who gives him gifts, like a Santa Claus. However, God wants to reveal Himself *inside* of the individual as his *life*—as being the One he needs, not just providing his needs.

Throughout His ministry, Jesus spoke of Himself as being the One we need. "I *am* the way—not just showing the way. I *am* the truth—I don't just give you the truth. I *am* the life—I don't just give you life apart from me. I *am* the bread. I *am* the resurrection and the life. I *am* the door, etc."

How can Christ reveal Himself as being the One we need, except by not giving us the things when we ask? He does this to cause us to realize our total dependence on *His life*, otherwise, we would remain babes.

As we choose to allow Christ's life to operate within us, this life will refine us. He is going to show us how to act as we yield to Him. He will work in us to love the unlovely. We don't need to pretend to love them, it will be real because we are depending on the law of life to operate through a conscious decision. We choose to believe,

> *I am crucified with Christ: nevertheless I live; yet not I, but Christ liveth in me: and the life which I now live in the flesh I live by the faith of the Son of God who loved, and gave himself for me* (Galatians 2:20).

He wants to live His life through us. He is not interested in what we can do. Ultimately, He is only interested in what we will let Him do through us. Therein lies the victory and the key.

We have to be subject to the Spirit at all times and never work independently of the Spirit. This does not happen over night; it is a growing process. According to Hebrews 5:14, *"... who by reason of use have their senses exercised to discern both good and evil."* As we learn to yield, to allow the Spirit to work through us, we will make mistakes, but the biggest mistake is to never step out at all.

The object of temptation is always to get us to do something apart from God. When we are going through a situation and God is taking us through trials and testing and we do not know which way to turn, we may be tempted to try again ourselves rather than trust. But the moment we try to solve our difficulty rather than trusting God, we are in the Enemy's territory. The divine way of victory does not permit us to do anything outside of Christ because as soon as we move in that direction we run into trouble. The devil-inspired natural inclination always carries us in the wrong direction.

Flying by Your Instruments

A close friend of mine, and one of the founders of the Christian Enrichment Family Camp, loaded himself and his family into their small plane. After they were in the air for fifteen minutes, a freak snowstorm struck, they crashed, and all of them were killed.

When the Department of Transport investigators came to interview me (since I was the last one to see them), they explained much of what they believed had happened. They told me that unless a person has been trained in instrument flying, when they get into a situation like a snowstorm and cannot see anything, they will often fail to believe their instruments and go according to natural inclinations.

They told me that they were 99 percent sure that my friend's natural inclination told him he was climbing when he was actually flying level. So he directed the plane to what he thought was level and headed down at 33 degrees, going 150 miles an hour. He fell back on relying on his senses and failed to believe his instruments.

Learning to walk by the Spirit is like learning to fly by instruments; we need to believe God's Truth, no matter what our senses tell us.

The Exchanged Life

This I say then, Walk in the Spirit, and ye shall not fulfil the lust of the flesh. For the flesh lusteth against the Spirit, and the Spirit against the flesh; and these are contrary the one to the other: so that ye cannot do the things that ye would. But if ye be led of the Spirit, ye are not under the law (Galatians 5:16-18).

It is not our fight. The Holy Spirit will do our fighting if we let Him: *"Walk in the Spirit, and ye shall not fulfil the lust of the flesh."* The answer is not to try to overcome the sin but to walk in the Spirit and let the Spirit do the work.

I am crucified with Christ: nevertheless I live; yet not I, but Christ liveth in me: and the life which I now live in the flesh I live by the faith of the Son of God who loved me, and gave himself for me (Galatians 2:20 NIV).

The fact is—if we draw on our old source, we will walk in defeat, but if we live by faith in the Son of God, who loved us and gave Himself for us, we are then victorious:

But they that wait upon the Lord shall renew their strength; they shall mount up with wings as eagles; they shall run, and not be weary; and they shall walk, and not faint (Isaiah 40:31).

The word "renew" in the Hebrew, as used in this passage can accurately be translated as "exchanged." We often think of the Christian life as the "changed life," but if this is where we stop, we won't progress beyond infancy. We have not only received a changed life, but God also gives us *His life*. This is the exchanged life.

Christ lives in us. Regeneration happens when the life of Christ is planted in us by the Holy Spirit at new birth, and we have a changed life. Reproduction is Christ's life reproduced in us progressively until we come into the very image of Jesus. This is the exchanged life.

Christ's life in us means victory because He is victorious. If we are praying for victory and are struggling to get victory, we won't attain it. For we do not fight *to gain* victory; we fight from the *position* of victory. Victory is ours because Jesus is Victor and He lives in us. The moment we strive for victory, we are off-base because we have lost sight of the fact of what we have in Christ Jesus.

The concept of sanctification means that every life should be holy. Holiness is Christ in us. If I am walking in the Spirit and truly recognize Who it is that lives in me, and I do not depend on my own strength and my own willpower, I am then walking in holiness:

But the fruit of the Spirit is love, joy, peace, longsuffering, gentleness, goodness, faith, meekness, temperance: against such there is no law (Galatians 5:22).

Listed here is the fruit of the Spirit. All those different types of fruit are listed, yet they are called the fruit (singular) of the Spirit because the fruit is Christ. We cannot get the fruit in pieces from God. When we receive Jesus, we get the whole package. God makes these things real to us by first increasing our awareness of our need for Him. For instance, if He puts us in a situation where we need patience, that situation will make us aware of our need for Him. He can then reveal to us that *He* is our patience; all we have to do is rest in Him and His Spirit will flow through us.

There is therefore now no condemnation to them which are in Christ Jesus, who walk not after the flesh, but after the Spirit. For the law of the Spirit of life in Christ Jesus hath made me free from the law of sin and death (Romans 8:1-2).

Another aspect of the exchanged life is to understand how to pull down *"the strong holds"* that our Enemy establishes in our lives.

For though we walk in the flesh, we do not war after the flesh: (For the weapons of our warfare are not carnal, but mighty through God to the pulling down of strong holds;) Casting down imaginations, and every high thing that exalteth itself against the knowledge of God, and bringing into captivity every thought to the obedience of Christ (II Corinthians. 10:3-5).

In Ephesians 6 we are given a description of the armour of God that we are to put on for our protection against the *"wiles of the devil"* and then *"stand."* However, in the above passage we are to use the weapons of our warfare to tear down the *"strong holds"* or fortresses that the Enemy has established or is trying to establish in our lives.

In Ephesians 6 we are told what the different parts of the armour are, but here we are not told what our *"weapons"* are. I heard Otto Koning on a teaching tape suggest what our weapons are which really made sense and witnessed with my spirit.

The first weapon is *"Rejoice in the Lord always: and again I say, Rejoice"* (Philippians. 4:4). When Paul gave this command to us, he was in prison and was probably chained to a guard. There was nothing in his circumstances that could produce joy. I am quite sure the Enemy tried to impose anxiety on Paul because in verse 6 he says *"Be careful* (anxious) *for nothing."* The Enemy always imposes negative reactions to trials and justifies the reactions. God wants us to respond by choosing to rejoice. When we choose to rejoice in trials we are exercising faith and therefore will experience growth.

The second weapon is, "In every thing give thanks: for this is the will of God in Christ Jesus concerning you" (I Thessalonians 5:18). The enemy wants us to complain and grumble like the Israelites did when they were faced with problems and thus waste the trials. God wants us to see trials as opportunities for growth and therefore, His will for us is to give thanks. To do this we again exercise faith, Paul says "And we know that all things work together for good to them that love God..." (Romans 8:28). Peter says, "That the trial of your faith, being much more precious than of gold that perisheth..." (I Peter 1:7).

No matter what difficulties we face, if we choose to rejoice and give thanks we are in God's will and are taking the wind out of the Enemy's sail and defeating him.

The third weapon is forgiveness. I have explained the three steps of forgiveness on pages 111 to 116. Again the Enemy will justify resentment and unforgiveness towards the person that has done something that hurt us in order to put us in bondage. However, if we choose to forgive and release the person we will be free, and the Enemy cannot build a *"strong hold"* in us.

The fourth and last weapon I want to mention is *"love."* When we choose to love the person who has hurt or offended us we are Christ-like and thus prevent the Enemy from having a *"strong hold"* in us.

Sometimes a person will tell me that he/she does not love his/her spouse anymore. I tell the person that if they are still living in the same house, they are neighbors and the Bible says you have to love your neighbor as yourself. If they have separated then at worst the spouse is an enemy and you are commanded to love your enemies. If we choose to love our neighbor as ourselves and choose to love our enemies, the Enemy cannot establish a foothold or fortress in our lives.

I trust you will be encouraged to recognize you do not need to be a victim of the Enemy, but can be an overcomer by faithfully applying these weapons.

These life-changing truths are clearly shown as accomplished facts in Romans 6-8. Romans 8:6 tells us, *"For to be carnally minded is death; but to be spiritually minded is life and peace."* This exchanged life is God's design and desire for us. It is my prayer that many will experience the truth expounded in this book.

NOTES

[1] G. Christian Weiss, *On Being a Real Christian* (Lincoln, NEBR: Back to the Bible Broadcast, 1951).

[2] "chastisement", The World Book Dictionary, 1972 ed.

[3] Stephen Kaung, *The Splendor of His Ways* (New York: Christian Fellowship Publishers, Inc., 1974).

[4] The author credits many of the truths described in chapter 11, "The Exchanged Life," to Watchman Nee, who has greatly influenced the teachings and ideas of the author. The following are books written by Watchman Nee: *The Normal Christian Life*, *Christ the Sum of All Spiritual Things*, and *Sit, Walk, Stand*.

Order Form

To order additional copies of *Answers and Hope for the Struggling Christian,* please use the form below.

Ordered by: *(please print)* _____

Name: _____

Address: _____

City: _____ Prov. / State: _____

Postal / Zip Code: _____ Tel.: _____

	Quantity	Each	Total
1-9 Books		$17.95	$
10+ Books		$14.95	$

Shipping : $_____
($4.00 plus $1.00 for each additional book.)

Total: $_____

Please enclose payment with your order.

Mail this form to: Henry Warkentin
                     Box 100
                     Caroline, AB, T0M 0M0
                     Canada

I would like to hear from you. It is my prayer that many hearts will experience the truth expounded in this book. Your comments, testimonial, or any other feedback can be valuable for future revisions. Please take a moment to write me.

You can e-mail me at: henryw@lfbc.net

Or write to: Henry Warkentin
Box 100
Caroline, Alberta, Canada
T0M 0M0